LOVING PEOPLE TOWARDS JESUS

Dub Everitt

www.lovingpeopletowardsJesus.com
Copyright © Dub Everitt and Welcome Church 2021

CONTENTS

Foreword   1

Introduction   5

PART 1: CARING & SHARING – Jesus' Mission for all His followers!

1. Sharing – The Great Commission   11
2. Caring – The Great Commandment   15
3. Power – The Extraordinary Through The Ordinary   19

PART 2: CARING – Loving people towards Jesus

4. Care Before You Share   27
5. Do Life Together   33
6. Precious People, Not Projects   37
7. Accept Others Just As They Are   43
8. Listening Opens The Door To Be Heard   47
9. Common Ground   53
10. Meet A Need   57
11. You Were Designed To Shine   61
12. You're God's Gift!   69
13. Patience Equals Perseverance   75
14. Look Up!   81
15. Placed there by God!   87

PART 3: STEP BY STEP – Loving people on Purpose

16. Loving People On Purpose	95
17. Don't Preach It Brother!	101
18. Meet The Family	107
19. Relational Momentum	113
20. The Power Of A Story	119
21. Be A Door Opener	125
22. Earn The Right To Invite	129
23. Be an Alphaholic!	135
24. The Harvest Is Plentiful!	143
25. You're Fruity!	149
26. Loving People Towards Jesus At Welcome Church	155
27. Here Am I. Send Me!	163

EPILOGUE 167

FOREWORD

During a meeting I had with the senior leaders of several churches in our town, representing a range of different denominations, I asked a question, "Are you seeing people saved and added to your church? Are you seeing people move from not knowing Jesus to making a decision to follow Jesus?"

The results were both encouraging and discouraging at the same time:

- They were encouraging because every church represented had seen at least one person come to faith in Jesus for the first time over the last year
- They were discouraging because the numbers were small: 1 here, 2 or 3 there, 5 or 6 somewhere else. In the words of one church leader: *"It's a slow but steady trickle, but it's certainly not revival"*

The conversation moved on to a discussion about *how* people were being reached. The Alpha Course was seen to have a significant place, and the importance of gathered Sunday worship meetings was highlighted too, but one thing was very clear, to quote one leader: *"It's just one person at a time, and it takes a lot more time and a lot more effort than we like to think it does. In fact it can take years for someone to respond"*

Another leader highlighted how people's view of the church and the Christian faith had changed, making the challenge greater than it used to be: "People used to tell me, 'I'm not interested because church is boring'. Now they don't just think church is boring; they think we're bigots who hate and oppress people. In reality they know nothing about what we believe, but they are certain that whatever it might be that we do actually believe, they don't like it and they are not interested."

Challenges certainly abound!

Despite all this, Jesus has a call on His church to make disciples of all nations. We have a message of life and hope - the amazing message of the gospel. The gospel is powerful and effective; it is the power of God for the salvation of everyone who believes. Let's have faith in the gospel and in our God who saves people.

This book is not in any way about changing the content of the gospel message, but it is about helping us think carefully about how to help people open up to receive this life changing message. Please read it prayerfully and let it shape what you do. This is a book that calls us all to take action.

As you read please know that Dub is someone who practices what he preaches; these principles have been forged through real life experience. There are people in our church today who have found a relationship with Jesus because they have been loved towards Him in some of the ways described in this book, by Dub himself and by many others.

When the book was first published we were working towards the public launch of our new Welcome Church building in the heart of Woking. Everyone in the church was given a copy of the book and encouraged to read it. The contents helped envision the whole church and led to people taking action. Relational momentum was built as friendships were made. Hundreds of guests came to the different church events that led up to our launch. At the launch itself we saw attendance numbers we would previously only have dreamed of, and our Sunday attendance grew very significantly as a result, with people exploring faith and coming to know Jesus for themselves.

What could Jesus do through us if we all stepped up to this exciting challenge?

Steve Petch, September 2021

INTRODUCTION

What's the worst experience you've had of someone trying to force their beliefs on you?

Or worse still:

What's the worst experience you've had of trying to force your beliefs onto someone else?

18 years ago I was a new Christian, full of enthusiasm and devoid of all tact – I know, I know, I'm still pretty limited in the area of tact now – but I had even less back then! I was convinced that, "God's got a good one here – He's gone and saved me, a top salesman. I'm going to sell Jesus to loads of people!"

So I set about the tactical process of trying to save others from their sins. Yes, you've guessed it, it didn't go well!

One evening we'd invited a couple, Natalie and Will[1], round to ours for dinner. Tanya, my wife, was looking forward to catching up with good friends, I however was ready to make the sale. After dinner we grabbed some more drinks and moved into the front room, and that's when I pulled out the 'preach' that I'd written for the occasion, a message taken from the Adrian Holloway book, 'The Shock of your Life'. I was going to scare our good friends into becoming Christians because ... well ... you never know ... *"they might die soon."*

The perfect after-dinner conversation!

---

[1] There are several stories in this book. Some of the names have been changed to preserve people's anonymity

I began by saying, *"I've written a letter to you guys, do you mind if I read it to you?"* They looked confused but agreed. Little did they know what was in store for them!

After reading about Jesus dying for their sins, and telling them that if they died without accepting Him they would go to hell, I looked up, ready to see if they wanted to pray 'the prayer' to accept Jesus with me.

Tanya looked incredibly embarrassed. Our guests were trying to see if they could jump out of the window. And then Will kindly said, *"Thank you for reading that. It's just not something I'm interested in. But just to reassure you, if it was something I was interested in then I would definitely be interested."*

You're right. What he said made no sense. But in that awkward moment that was his amazing attempt to say something kind as opposed to what he might have said.

Bizarrely, Tanya seemed less keen on evangelism after that evening.

Now I know your story of evangelism gone wrong isn't going to be as bad as mine, but most Christians have horror stories of trying to share our faith and it all going pear-shaped. These experiences can scar us, leaving us less likely to share our faith the next time. We may still speak about Jesus with other Christians but, before we know it, months and years may have passed since we last shared our faith with someone who isn't a Christian.

Our lives get split into 2 distinct parts: our 'Christian bubble' of church and Life Group, and the 'normal' parts of our lives ... and never the twain shall meet.

Does that have to be our story? Is that *supposed to* be our story?

Do we just ignore the bits of the Bible where Jesus tells us, *"Go and make disciples,"* and *"You will be my witnesses,"* and instead do the other parts of the Christian life such as attending church meetings, being nice and trying not to swear?

This book is written around both Jesus' insistence that making disciples is central to every Christian life and my own observations of how Jesus is changing people's lives around us – people from all sorts of backgrounds and starting points. I believe this book can be a great encouragement to you that:

- *Jesus IS calling us to lead others to Him*
- *He IS going to give us all we need to do that*
- *The model He has for us in 21st Century Britain ISN'T based around awkward preaching to those who don't want to hear, but is actually based around the enjoyment of building friendships with people*

In this book we'll look at the principles of how God will equip us to draw people to Jesus, and I'll share lots of stories of people I've seen come to faith. I believe this book will lead you on the exciting adventure of loving people around you towards Jesus … if you're open to it!

PART 1

CARING & SHARING – JESUS' MISSION FOR ALL HIS FOLLOWERS!

Let's face it, literally everything Jesus said was great! He spoke healing over some, He spoke forgiveness over others, He revealed the love of God through what He said as well as did. He literally spoke *"the words of eternal life."* (John 6v68)

But there are two great things in particular that He wants every one of us, His followers, to underline in our bibles and work out through our lives - His Great Commission and His Great Commandment.

In this first part, we're going to reflect on what these two Great's are and consider what they mean for us individually and as church communities. And once we've considered them both and seen what an impossibly tall order they are, we will then breathe a huge sigh of relief as we hear of how Jesus wants to empower us to fulfil them!

Welcome to Part 1 of Loving People Towards Jesus.

1

SHARING – THE GREAT COMMISSION

Jesus came to them and said, "All authority in heaven and on earth has been given to me. Therefore go and make disciples of all nations, baptising them in the name of the Father and of the Son and of the Holy Spirit, and teaching them to obey everything I have commanded you. And surely I am with you always, to the very end of the age"

Matthew 28v18-20

Jesus commanded us to *"Go and make disciples."* This command wasn't just a small sidebar to the role He's given His followers or a calling for the special, gifted few. This command seems to be the RAISON D'ETRE for His church; the primary mission His church is built around. To *"go and make disciples"* is something Jesus calls every church and every Christian to.

Often called "The Great Commission," this calling is the big "WHAT" of Jesus' church. We are called to tell the world around us about Jesus and to call people to follow Him.

Pastor Rick Warren says, "God wants His lost children found. Nothing matters more than that."

And although it can feel like "Com-mission Impossible," Jesus assures us that there is a *"Great Harvest,"* and that as we get involved we will *"bear much fruit"* – which means we will see lots of people coming to faith in Him.

"I will build my church," He tells us … and He is going to use US to do it!

Frustratingly, Jesus' Great Commission gives us a message that needs to be SPOKEN. Romans 10v13-15 explains,

> *"Everyone who calls on the name of the Lord will be saved.*
> *How, then, can they call on the one they have not believed in?*
> *And how can they believe in the one of whom they have not heard?*
> **And how can they hear without someone preaching to them?**
> *And how can anyone preach unless they are sent?*
> *As it is written: 'How beautiful are the feet of those who bring good news!'"*

Often called "evangelism," sharing our faith is perhaps the number one thing that most Christians are scared of in life! Evangelism is defined in the Cambridge dictionary as, *"the activity of persuading people to become Christians."* The gospel is not something that people can just work out for themselves; it's a factual message, based on historical events, given by Jesus to His followers and it needs to be spoken out loud!

For the sake of simplicity, and to try to remove the fear out of the whole thing, we're going to call evangelism **"Sharing"** – sharing our faith with others.

I believe that every follower of Jesus wants their friends, family, neighbours and work colleagues to follow Jesus too – we just struggle to know how to tell them about Him!

As I look at some of my "car crash" moments of sharing my faith, and as you think about yours, it's perhaps no wonder we want to zip our mouths, keep our faith to ourselves and just talk about other things with those we do life with.

Here are a few of the things we sometimes say to ourselves as reasons we don't share our faith:
- "I won't know what to say"
- "I don't have all the answers"
- "I don't know enough"
- "It's not my gift"
- "I'll get tongue-tied"
- "I'm too embarrassed"
- "They won't be interested"
- "I'M TOO SCARED!!"

The Southern Baptist Church in the USA did a comprehensive survey about whether or not their members shared their faith, and this is what they discovered. Out of those Christians who were born into a Southern Baptist Church family, were raised within the church, met and married someone from the church, and went on to raise their children within the Southern Baptist Church, only 10% of them said they would *possibly* share their faith with others, and 90% of them said they would never share their faith with anyone else. Ever.

Isn't that an incredible and shocking statistic?

And isn't it a little closer to our reality than we'd care to admit?

But here's a key question: What if sharing our faith isn't just for the extroverts who sing hymns down the shopping aisles? What if it's possible to share our faith in a genuine way that's not awkward or painful, and can lead to others drawing closer to Jesus? What if within our churches, our statistics were that 90% of us WERE sharing our faith instead of weren't?

And to make this personal, what if every one of us could see people in our lives coming to faith in Jesus? What if YOU could see people in your life coming to faith in Jesus? How would you feel about seeing that happen?

I've realised over the years that we can look at sharing our faith as such a high bar that it causes us to feel we can't reach it, and sometimes this height we imagine we have to reach can be down to how we feel we have to deliver the message. I've also discovered that the 'HOW' Jesus is calling us to share our faith, is actually really different from what most of us think. His calling is actually far less daunting and far more fun than we imagine, and the rewards are simply indescribable as we see people we care about come to faith in Jesus!

The issue is not the MESSAGE; the issue is actually our METHOD.

2

CARING – THE GREAT COMMANDMENT

Jesus replied,
"Love the Lord your God with all your heart
and with all your strength and with all your mind.
This is the first and greatest commandment.
And the second is like it: Love your neighbour as yourself."

Matthew 22v37-39

If the Great Commission – sharing our faith – is the 'WHAT', then the 'Great Commandment' is the 'HOW'.

That fateful night I described in the Introduction to this book, I was sharing my faith because I cared for our friends. I wanted them to have what I had – a relationship with Jesus, the most amazing, life-transforming person they'd ever encounter.

There is a well-known phrase, *'Sharing is caring'*. Sadly I'd convinced myself that *"sharing my faith without consideration for the other person was still caring."* I ploughed on, forcing the Bible down their throats until they wanted to vomit. But Jesus' message is a message of love. The God who is love is reaching out to people across this messed up world, not treating us as our sins deserve but instead, in His great love, mercy and grace, offering perfect forgiveness and a relationship with Himself.

But not only is Jesus' message about love, His method is a method of love too. In John 15v12 Jesus said, *"This is my commandment, that you love one another as I have loved you"*. In all that we do, in every interaction we have, we are called to lead with love.

In the New Testament the world's greatest evangelist, the Apostle Paul, who led thousands and thousands of people across the known world to faith in Jesus, reminds us that anything we do without love is worthless:

"If I speak in the tongues of men and angels but have not love, I am only a resounding gong or a clanging cymbal. If I have the gift of prophecy and can fathom all mysteries and all knowledge, and if I have a faith that can move mountains, but have not love, I am nothing. If I give all I possess to the poor and surrender my body to the flames, but have not love, I gain nothing." 1 Corinthians 13v1-3

These words are profound, so let's dwell on them for a moment. Things we consider incredibly "spiritual" such as speaking in tongues, prophesying and having faith that can move mountains are WORTHLESS if they're done without love!

So when it comes to what is 'spiritual', love comes out as number one. Anything else that we may feel is at the height of Christian maturity is actually worth no more than chucking on the rubbish heap if it's done without love.

Jesus' PRIMARY CALL to us as His followers is to what Paul calls, *"the most excellent way"* of love – love for God and love for people – this is His 'Great Commandment'. We will call this command to love people, **'Caring'**.

Leading with love is the most spiritual thing we can do. I don't know about you, but doesn't that feel incredibly releasing? You and I don't have to be soapbox preachers, hammering others whilst wishing the ground would open up and swallow us.

As we lead with love, having faith that the God who transforms our lives is still at work, drawing people to Himself, you and I can see our friends and loved ones come to faith as we love them towards Jesus.

"How do I generate this love?", you may be asking. "I've got enough going on and don't have the capacity to love others!" Well the answer to this is good news, which our next chapter will tell us.

3

POWER – THE EXTRAORDINARY THROUGH THE ORDINARY

"Do not leave Jerusalem, but wait for the gift my Father promised, which you have heard me speak about. For John baptized with water, but in a few days you will be baptized with the Holy Spirit... You will receive power when the Holy Spirit comes on you; and you will be my witnesses."

Acts 1v4, 5, 8

I wonder how Jesus' disciples felt after they saw Him raised from the dead? They went from desperation at seeing Him die on the cross to utter joy as He met with them again 3 days later! I can imagine the desire of Peter and the others would have been to tell everyone they could that their Rabbi had proven who He was by rising again. This was the biggest news EVER!

And Jesus' desire absolutely was that His followers would tell the world about Him. We've already looked at His words recorded at the end of the gospel of Matthew: *"Go and make disciples of all nations..."* – go and tell the world about me!

Yet, at the beginning of the book of Acts, Jesus is recorded saying these words – *"Do not leave Jerusalem, but wait...."* What? But we've got a mission to complete Jesus. We need to tell the world about you! Wait??!! Wait for what?

"... wait for the gift my Father promised, which you have heard me speak about. For John baptised *with water, but in a few days you will be baptized with the Holy Spirit...* You will receive power when the Holy Spirit comes on you; and you will be my witnesses." (Acts 1v4,5,8).

What a fascinating command Jesus made to His disciples – which is also a command He makes to you and me today too! Don't go anywhere, don't do anything, don't try to tell people about me – yet. First, be filled with the Holy Spirit, receive the power He will fill you with – and then you'll be my witnesses.

My own life for years after becoming a Christian was one of hard work! I was sure I'd convince loads of my friends, colleagues, and teammates to become Christians. It was a big group of potential converts, and I had a real drive to tell them about Jesus and try and save them all!

I was the hardest grafter you'd see in church life, one of the most outgoing wannabe evangelists we had, and yet after a full decade I was the worst Christian salesman on earth! My record after ten years – I'd spoken to probably 200 different people about my faith and had seen zero friends become Christians as a result. How's that for a hit rate? How's that for demoralising?

I felt like just giving up on the thankless and fruitless task of drawing anyone to Jesus. I remember praying a prayer of utter frustration to God, *"I CAN'T DO THIS GOD. I CAN'T SAVE ANYONE!!!"*

I just sensed a quiet, gentle response, deep down inside. "I'm glad you've worked that out son. Can you do it my way now?"

Ouch. So many years of hard graft and I was doing it all wrong. And yet, not a rebuke from God but a loving re-direct for me.

What was the problem? I was trying to do something NO HUMAN can do in their own strength. A person coming to faith in Jesus is a SPIRITUAL MOMENT. It's the Holy Spirit who reveals Jesus to people. Jesus reminded us of this in John 3v6, *"Flesh gives birth to flesh, but the Spirit gives birth to spirit."* And there was I, a human in my own human strength, trying to achieve a spiritual outcome that only the Holy Spirit is appointed to do. It was a hard lesson over so many years. But it's been a lesson well learned.

I've learnt how BOTH 'caring' and 'sharing' to see people come to faith through me WON'T HAPPEN unless I'm filled with the Holy Spirit – but as the Holy Spirit fills me I will receive the God-given ability to CARE, fulfilling Jesus' Great Commandment to love, and to SHARE, to help people encounter Jesus!

While the verses at the top of this chapter show us that we can only SHARE effectively – be Jesus' witnesses – once we've been filled with the Holy Spirit, the letter to the Romans in the bible also reminds us that we can only truly CARE – to really love people – once we've been filled with the Holy Spirit. *"God's love has been poured out into our hearts through the Holy Spirit, who has been given to us"* (Romans 5v5). The only way you and I will find the capacity to love others begins by receiving Jesus' great love for us. This will cause love to bubble up in our hearts – firstly for Jesus and secondly for what Jesus loves – other sinful people all around us. As we receive more and more of this vast, selfless, heavenly love, it'll flow in us and then out to others.

So, if you want God to draw people to Jesus through you, Jesus has a crystal-clear instruction – don't do anything in your own strength. First be filled with the Holy Spirit, and you'll then be equipped and empowered to love people and to be His witnesses.

When you've received the Holy Spirit, been empowered by Him, you can be confident that Jesus' light will shine through you, that God's love will pour out of you, that when people encounter you they're encountering the presence of God through you. I can't overstate the significance of this. My decade of painful fruitlessness shows me I can't do any of this in my own strength, and the following 9 years has shown me the night and day difference being filled with the Holy Spirit makes in each and every encounter I have with someone.

As I look around my life right now, I can see my outreach has gone from zero to becoming more and more fruitful; I have seen lots of people around me come to faith in Jesus, and there are lots of other people I'm connected to who are being drawn closer by Him, step by step, as I help them along their journey. I've gone from foolish self-confidence to an ever-growing confidence in God being at work through me over these years as I've seen all sorts of people from all sorts of starting places come to faith in Jesus.

Do you desire to see people in your life saved by Jesus? Would you love to know people are encountering the love of God every time they interact with you? Would you love to be used by Him in drawing others to faith in Him? Well, let me encourage you to receive Jesus' instruction for yourself as your very first step – stop, wait, and be filled with the Holy Spirit, being confident that God's plan for your life is good and that He is able to do things in you and through you that are simply impossible in your own strength!

QUESTIONS

Where do you lack confidence in seeing people come to faith?

What would Jesus want you to learn about the significance of being filled with the Holy Spirit in order to fulfil both His Great Commandment to Love and His Great Commission to lead people to Him?

Is there anything you want to say to God at his point? Tell God how you feel about past disappointments. Ask Him to fill you with faith in His promises to work through you. Turn all of your thoughts into prayer.

Ask God to fill you with the Holy Spirit. It's often helpful to ask another Christian to pray for you to be filled with the Holy Spirit.

PART 2

CARING – LOVING PEOPLE TOWARDS JESUS

So we've got our foundation of hearing of how Jesus is calling us to fulfil His Great Commandment to love, and we've heard how the Holy Spirit is the one who will supernaturally enable us to do it.

This Part of the book is where we'll unpack this as we read biblical truth after biblical truth alongside story after story of HOW He will do this through us as we lean in to Him and reach out to others. As I'm writing this introduction, I'm reminded of the words of a worship song title: *"Yet not I, but through Christ in me."* As we'll see throughout this section, these song words sum up so well what will happen as you and I reach out and love others with the love Jesus has put in us.

I believe that, no matter how 'ordinary' you feel, this section could be life-changing as you read it and choose to believe Jesus, the One who wants to do the extraordinary through you.

4

CARE BEFORE YOU SHARE

"Because we loved you so much, we were delighted to share with you not only the gospel of God but our lives as well."

1 Thessalonians 2v8

Times change. Things that people once swore by can become defunct over time, or at the least less effective. Listening to music for example. People still love to listen to music as much as anyone ever has, but the method by which they listen is completely different today. Take the audio cassette tape. *"The what?"* cries everyone under the age of 25. Exactly.

Our church has been around for over 140 years and, although the gospel does not change, the culture we live in has changed a lot during that time, so our ways of reaching out to people need to change too. In generations past, when we were a "Christian nation", you could put a soapbox in a town square and preach the gospel, a crowd would gather and some might come to faith. I'm pretty sure that if we were to do that today any crowds gathering would either be holding placards or throwing rotten tomatoes.

I've experienced the reality of this old method in a new culture. As a church we've held public outreach events in the past in the form of a church service. We had worship music with a small group of people from the church singing along, followed by a couple of gospel messages. We did this in the open air, right in the centre of town. I went along to hand out flyers at one of these events when I first joined our church, and the look of horror on people's faces as they ran in the opposite direction from us 'happy clappers' will stay in my memory for a long time. After two hours I was still holding 198 of my 200 flyers. A method that was once effective was perhaps now doing more harm than good.

When we changed our Christmas Outreach in Woking the following year to a mini Fun-Day, with free hot dogs and mulled wine alongside Face Painting and a professional musician performing 'busker-style' carols, around 1,000 people happily took a Carol Service flyer along with their hot dog, and we received hundreds of comments about what an amazing event Welcome Church had put on. We then saw people from that event come along to our Carol Service and some signed up for Alpha (a great, friendly course based around a meal where over 8 weeks you look at some of the key aspects of Jesus and the Christian faith).

This holds true in the small as well as the big. Someone told me that they always invite the whole of their street to our Carol Service each year. Amazed, I wanted to find out more. *"That's brilliant,"* I said, *"How do you make the invites? Do you have your neighbours over for a Christmas drink and then invite them?" "Oh no,"* they replied, *"we don't actually know them. We just put flyers through their letterboxes.* **But none of them ever come!"**

Contrast this with Florence. Florence instigated a community BBQ on her local green. She put invitations to her BBQ through over 100 of her neighbours' doors inviting them to come and join her. Over 40 came, and 2 decided to come to church with her the following day. What's the difference? Leading with love and being involved in people's lives. Caring for others really does make the world of difference.

YOU DON'T NEED TO BE A PREACHER OR A PROFESSIONAL!

My observations of how God is working and how people respond is this: in the United Kingdom in the 21st Century, it is paramount that we **CARE BEFORE WE SHARE**. Contrary to some 'religious' opinion, caring for others is not less spiritual than sharing the gospel. Fulfilling Jesus' Great Commandment is not secondary in value.

There's a great quote from Teddy Roosevelt, former President of the United States, who coined a really insightful phrase, when he said:

> *"People don't care how much you know,
> until they know how much you care!"*

This is such a profound insight, particularly from someone who could have expected people to listen to him because of the position he held. And today, in 21st Century Britain, this phrase proves so true for us as Christians who have been given a message to share. Cold-call Christianity regularly proves to be a great turn-off to the people God has placed around us; what gets people's attention is authentic kindness and friendship.

Sadly, there are lots of people who have a negative view of Christianity, and these negative views can have many different roots. Some people are negative because of judgemental Christian attitudes they've encountered, some because of media articles describing Christians as 'narrow-minded' or 'bigoted' and some may have had church experiences that they found to be 'boring' or 'irrelevant'. The key thing that will dispel people's negative views is not someone 'preaching' at them; it's the authentic kindness and love of Jesus being shown to them through one of His followers.

Saint Francis of Assisi (allegedly) said, "Preach the Gospel at all times. When necessary, use words." Now he's not saying, "Never speak about Jesus." But he is saying, "Your actions speak louder than your words. Your kindness opens a window for others to see the heart of the One you follow." His words are a call for us to care before we share.

The great news is, whereas you may feel unqualified to be an evangelist, caring is NOT just for the 'professionals'; it's NOT only for Bible experts or for those with theology degrees; it's NOT only for extroverts. "Caring" is simply giving time, building friendships, showing love, having fun together, meeting a need, being there for someone and building community. And this is something that EVERY Jesus follower can do and is called to do.

Personally I'm relieved that Jesus' primary call on me is to care for people. The thought of going back to that dreadful evening of 'preaching' to our friends after dinner turns my stomach, but to reach out and to care is something I can do, it's something you can do, and it can make the world of difference.

This part of the book is all about fulfilling Jesus' Great Commandment to love others. It contains some observations and some stories, and I hope it will be a great encouragement that you are called and gifted to do the most spiritual thing in the world: to love others towards Jesus.

When it comes to seeing people come to faith in Jesus, it's really important to remember that Jesus' desire to save people today is as strong as ever. 2,000 years ago He said, *"the harvest is plentiful,"* and that harvest is still plentiful today here in the UK, as well as in the rest of the world. His means for reaching people is the same as it's always been: through His followers. Yes! He wants to reach people through you and me.

Perhaps the negative press that the church in the UK has received over the last few years is an important wake up call for us all to remember to live out this amazing Great Commandment of Jesus to love people. Perhaps we've either been too focussed on preaching at people, or simply been too busy with church life. Or perhaps we've been too tied up with looking after Number 1 to fulfil His Commandment to care. Either way, it's time we re-embraced the call of Jesus to go and love those around us!

5

DO LIFE TOGETHER

"All the believers were together and had everything in common. Selling their possessions and goods, they gave to anyone as he had need... They broke bread in their homes and ate together with glad and sincere hearts.
And the Lord added to their number daily those who were being saved."

Acts 2v44-47

In their wedding vows, people declare to their spouse, *"For better or worse, in sickness and in health."* They declare, *"All that I have I share with you."* From their hearts to their homes, their mattress to their money, it's an amazing promise of generosity and of valuing the other person.

Jesus calls us all to live out this high call of love, not just to a spouse but to all the people He's placed around us (with the exception of sharing our mattresses!) How do you feel about Jesus' call to this level of generosity and love to others, for better or worse? Those who are married will know that it can be enough of a struggle just to have this level of generosity towards one person!

"All that I have I share with my spouse, everyone else can sort themselves out!" is not the life Jesus calls us to. Jesus' call to His followers is a call to generosity in sharing what we've got with others liberally and extravagantly. He reminds us that our true provider is

God Himself who *"knows what you need before you even ask";* the God who owns the whole earth and everything in it, and who promises to provide for His children.

As we come to believe this is true about God, it loosens our purse-strings, helps us unbolt our front door and helps us step into generosity towards others. In a world where it's 'dog eat dog', a Jesus follower is playing by different rules – the Heavenly rules of generosity. This can make a huge difference in other people's lives.

TO OPEN UP YOUR LIFE, OPEN UP YOUR FRONT DOOR!

In Jesus' time and across the Middle East today you would know someone cares by whether they will give you the honour of coming to eat with you in your home. When Jesus said to Zacchaeus, *"Quick, come down. I must be a guest in your home today,"* it wasn't Jesus being cheeky and barging in where He was not wanted; Jesus was actually saying, *"Zacchaeus I see you, I value you and I want to bring you honour."* (see Luke 19v1-10)

The impact on Zacchaeus of Jesus honouring him in this way was life-transforming: he changed his dodgy ways, gave money to the poor and followed Jesus, leading Jesus to say, *"Today salvation has come to this house. For the Son of Man came to seek and to save what was lost."*

It's similar in 21st Century Britain but usually works the opposite way around: we know that someone values us when they open their front door and invite us in. There is a saying that, *"An Englishman's home is his castle"*. This speaks of a home where the fences are high, the drawbridge is up and you're not invited in. But when a Christian opens their door wide and welcomes someone in, it says loud and clear, *"I value you; you matter!"*

When our family were moving to Woking at the end of 2014 for me to work for Welcome Church, we prayed for a home within walking distance of the right school. God gave us a perfect house which was the 2nd closest to the back gate of both the Lower and Junior Schools that Tanya wanted to send our children to! This was a wonderful answer to prayer, and also a great opportunity for us to build community with lots of families.

One of my favourite things is having people over, and the location of our home is perfect for it. We've had the privilege of having lots of children over for playdates with our kids, Tanya has had loads of Mums over for coffee, we've held World Cup Football BBQ's for school Dads and families, and we've had all sorts of socials with lots of different families. It's meant that our home is regularly busy, and we're doing life with loads of other people.

Tanya and I alongside Kirk and Helen became really good friends with Bridget and Matt and their girls through school. Through our friendships, they began connecting with Welcome Church, and even attended a Bible camp weekend with our church. This is a message Bridget sent me on the way home from that weekend:

"I feel blessed that you are all part of our lives and have welcomed us so openly, quirks and all!"

You'll read Bridget's husband Matt's amazing story of coming to faith in the 'Relational Momentum' chapter.

In a world where increasing numbers of people are suffering from loneliness, where communities are fragmented and genuine friendships are hard to find, doing life with others in a way that shows how much you care will be such a blessing. And remember, through this simple act, **God will be at work through you**, as we will see in the pages ahead.

YOU'RE WORTH BEING FRIENDS WITH

If someone is precious, they're worth our time. They're not people we're just wanting to give information to about God so that we feel like we've done our duty; they're people we want to be with, care for, help, support, laugh and have fun with, and even comfort and grieve with.

Don't be too quick to invite them to church! As you build genuine friendships of love and care with precious people, an out of the blue invite to church too soon may not be what your friend needs. With preconceptions abounding about what Christians are like, allowing yourself to spend a good amount of time building a great friendship with someone is the perfect start to them getting to know a Jesus follower.

As you build your friendships, it's amazing and so encouraging to remember that they're encountering God's love through you.

Remember, **trust can't be rushed**. The time to make an invite will come – don't feel you need to rush it!

6

PRECIOUS PEOPLE NOT PROJECTS

"When Jesus saw the crowds, he had compassion on them, because they were harassed and helpless, like sheep without a shepherd."

Matthew 9v36

I hadn't caught up with my neighbour for a couple of months when they dropped me a message saying, *"Let's catch up for a coffee soon."* Our church had just published the details of our next Alpha Course and this looked like a great opportunity, so my text reply was, *"Coffee sounds good. Alpha is starting soon - can I sign you up?"* Their reply came swiftly, *"Thank you, no."*

The issue? They'd asked for coffee and I had tried to bring them to church. They could have been left thinking, *"Dub is too busy to spend time with me; he just wants to make me like him"*.

Everyone who encountered Jesus experienced someone who valued them highly; God's Son made time for other people. In the Bible we often see Jesus adjusting His plans based on other's needs. John, one of Jesus' disciples felt this love so deeply that he refers to himself in his gospel as, "the disciple Jesus loved." Wherever He went, people who encountered Jesus felt the same way.

Jesus launched the greatest mission this world will ever see: to draw people back to God. This continues to be the world's most successful mission, with over 2 billion people alive today declaring themselves to be Jesus followers. Yet Jesus' method was never about the masses at the expense of the individual or aiming at a quick sale at the expense of transforming a heart. Jesus *loved people* because he saw them as precious.

The word compassion in the above verse speaks, in the original language of a deep stirring in the bowels! Jesus saw the crowds and felt deep emotions for them right to his very core, and that was his motivation for reaching out to people one by one, meeting them at their point of need, and telling them the good news that, *"God loves you so much that He has sent me for you."*

SEE THE MASTERPIECE

The old adage is that something is worth what someone is willing to pay for it. Jesus showed the value of every human being by paying the highest price possible - His own life. Peter, one of Jesus' disciples, explains that, *"God paid a ransom to save you from the empty life you inherited from your ancestors. And the ransom he paid was not mere gold or silver. It was the precious blood of Christ."* (1 Peter 1v18-19)

Jesus treated everyone He met with kindness and grace. He had compassion on those He saw were struggling and moved to meet them at their point of need. And He then paid the highest price for them as He shed His blood on the cross for them.

You could never ever accuse Jesus of seeing people as a project, and He never judged by outward appearances, whether rich or poor. He saw everyone as they truly are: precious, carefully crafted by their Creator, and worth giving everything for.

An amazing quote by Michelangelo brings Jesus' view of people to life so well: "In every block of marble I see a statue as plain as though it stood before me, shaped and perfect in attitude and action. I have only to hew away the rough walls that imprison the lovely apparition to reveal it to the other eyes as mine see it."

Michelangelo saw a masterpiece where others only saw a rough block of marble. And Jesus sees a masterpiece created by God the Master Craftsman where we can sometimes only see a mess. When we look at others, what do we see? And when we connect with others, what do we feel? Every single encounter with another person, if we're to be like the One we follow, needs to be motivated by love.

FEELINGS SPEAK LOUDER THAN WORDS

Did you know that only 7% of communication is verbal? The other 93% of communication consists of our body language (55%) and our tone of voice (38%). (These are the results of a study on non-verbal communication by Dr. Mehrabian in the 1960's). You'll know this is true if you've spoken to someone who is passive aggressive; their words may be 'kind' on paper, but their attitude and anger speak so loudly it's almost deafening.

Very often people know how we FEEL about them long before we open our mouths, and regardless of the words we use. So, although words are important, having love for someone in your heart is far more important. Do you have love for the people God has placed around you? If so, they're encountering His love every time they encounter you.

Elaine had been coming to our "Welcome Meal"[2] for over a decade. She'd been an alcoholic for longer than that time, and her current address was a sleeping bag on the steps of the building next to our church. The one thing she did every week without fail was to come to our Friday lunchtime "Welcome Meal" – in her world of feeling like everyone judged her, it was the one place she experienced people treating her in a way that showed how precious she was.

Our Welcome Meal team are full of love and kindness. Ann leads the team, and really does lead by example in the way she cares for all of our guests. She regularly would look out for Elaine, sit with her and encourage her. Elaine was a self-confessed atheist but would really enjoy the love that these Christians gave her.

When Elaine was considering quitting drinking, Ann encouraged her that she could do it, always offering to pray for her. After detox, when she was receiving so much love and encouragement from people across the church, she started to ask for prayer rather than waiting for it to be offered. She was experiencing the love of the God she didn't believe in.

Elaine joined Ann's Life Group[3] and was wrapped up in love by people across the group. And when Alpha next came around, Elaine said yes and joined. She's now done three consecutive Alpha courses, opening up more and more to God slowly but surely. It all began with her being shown how precious she is.

---

[2] Welcome Meal was a weekly lunch and support group that our church provided for people in need for around 25 years

[3] Life Groups are our small groups that meet regularly to support, encourage and 'do life' with each other

The challenge for us sometimes can be that through our busyness and 'to do' lists, we can feel like we're all out of love as well as time. If that's how you're feeling, what do you do? Well, trying harder to say the right things isn't going to work! There's one simple thing to do: go back to the source of love and have your love tank re-filled. The Bible reminds us that, *"We love because God first loved us,"* (1 John 4v19) and that, *"God has poured his love into our hearts through the Holy Spirit."* (Romans 5v5).

Your Heavenly Father, the source of all love, is right with you waiting to re-fill you with His love. So why don't you pause, put this book down, and pray? Thank God for His never-ending love towards you and ask Him to re-fill your heart with His love for others right now. As you pause, have faith that just as you're breathing in air at this moment, you're also receiving His love to soften your heart, to re-fill and refresh you.

God's love in you is the motivation for loving others. Allow your life to be like a funnel, continually receiving God's love and continually pouring it out to others that God has placed all around you. You're precious to God, and they are too, which is why He's blessed them by putting YOU in their lives.

7

ACCEPT OTHERS JUST AS THEY ARE

Jesus said to them, "If any one of you is without sin, let him cast the first stone at her." At this, those who heard began to go away one at a time, the older ones first, until only Jesus was left, with the woman still standing there. "Woman, where are they? Has no one condemned you?" "No one, sir," she said. "Then neither do I condemn you," Jesus declared. "Go now and leave your life of sin."

John 8v7-11

Acceptance of others is essential to our calling. Jesus makes it clear that our role is not to judge others, but to love them, and this means accepting them just as they are.

The more religious among us may feel that, "I can't condone behaviour that is sinful!" We need to understand that acceptance is not saying, "I approve of your lifestyle." Acceptance is saying, "I love and value you as a person made in God's image." And this is part of Jesus' call to us as His followers.

"But," we may think, "it's very important that they know their behaviour is out of line with God's standards. If I don't point out their sin, how will they know they need to repent?"

But what if the first and most important thing that Jesus wants people to know is that GOD LOVES THEM.

The most famous Bible verse in the world is John 3v16, "For God so loved the world that He gave His one and only Son, that whosoever believes in Him shall not perish but have everlasting life". I think it's crucial that we also remember the next verse too, v17, "For God did not send His Son into the world to condemn the world, but to save the world through Him."

If it wasn't Jesus' mission to condemn people, it's certainly not ours. Unfortunately, Christians can sometimes feel that clearly pointing out someone's sin to them is the key first step. We may think that once they feel bad enough about their sin, we can then tell them the good news that Jesus died to bring forgiveness for those sins.

There may have been times and cultures in history when this worked, but in our culture today I believe that this is a path to putting people off our message. *"You're a sinner, and you need cleaning up!"* may be true, but it will leave people feeling condemned rather than drawn towards Jesus and the 'good news' He came to bring, shutting them down to the gospel rather than opening them up to it.

Lots of people's lives are out of step with the life Jesus calls us to. The reality is, this is true for people whether or not they're Christians! In fact when we compare our 'goodness' to God's standards, every human being is infinitely closer to each other in sinfulness than we are to God's 'holiness'. We're all a work in progress.

So isn't it interesting, strange or (more accurately) sad when a Christian looks down their nose at someone else because of their lifestyle or behaviour? If you've been prone to judging other people's behaviours, you're not the first person of faith to do so. In the verses above, the 'religious' people, who believed they were doing God's will, had judged the woman as 'sinful' and 'worthy of judgement,' even to the point of death by stoning.

But look at the sharp contrast between their attitude to her and how Jesus treated her. They had rocks in their hands; Jesus had compassion in his eyes. They spoke judgement and anger; Jesus spoke love and mercy. They wanted to end her life; Jesus pointed her towards a new life.

Some church historians suggest that this woman was Mary Magdalene, who became a devoted follower of Jesus. Whether this is true or not, the impact of Jesus showing acceptance to her – a key part of love – was life-changing, and this story still affects people deeply today.

Jesus calls us to be like Him in our interactions with others and when we are offering kindness, support and love, it impacts people deeply. Remember, acceptance is not saying, *"I approve of what you do"*, but it is saying, *"I will show you love just as you are"* – and this is exactly how God treats us. Reaching out to others has to start here.

Betty was a Mum on the schoolgate. When she upset a group of other Mums, it seemed to her as though everyone turned their back on her. One particular morning after drop-off was really painful for Betty when she asked the other Mums why they were ignoring her, why they were cutting her out of their group, why they were arranging socials without her. One by one these Mums turned and said to her, *"I can't be doing with this…", "I've got to go…", "I've got enough going on right now…"*

Betty was left there on her own – except for three other parents, all of whom were Christians from Welcome Church. These three gathered around her, supported her, and helped her know she was loved.

This led to the 3 families making time to keep connecting with Betty, which led to her connecting with their Life Group, before she eventually came to Welcome Church on a Sunday and started doing Alpha. She now describes her new-found church friends, especially her Life Group, as her 'family'.

When we remove judgement and instead offer acceptance we're being like Jesus, and it really does draw people to Him.

8

LISTENING OPENS THE DOOR TO BE HEARD

"Take note of this: Everyone should be quick to listen, slow to speak and slow to become angry."

James 1v19

A few years ago, when I was a Sales Director, we'd just taken on a new Sales Rep, Ken. I was spending a couple of days with him as he drove me around his patch to meet customers and for me to show him the ropes. Whilst driving, we went past a church with a poster outside. His comments surprised me… *"Those bl***y Christians! They're all the same – hypocrites trying to force their beliefs on other people. I bl***y hate Christians!"*

PRESS PAUSE. What do you do in a moment like that?

I know what I felt an urge to do - I wanted to push back. I wanted to say, "I'm a Christian. What you're saying is really unfair. Loads of Christians aren't how you're describing…"

But if I'd done that, what would've happened? Probably 1 of 2 things. Either we would've had a bit of a head-to-head, arguing the toss. Or he would most likely have thought, *"Oops, I've upset my new boss,"* and felt he needed to apologise and shut the conversation down. Either way, it wouldn't have gone well, and wouldn't have helped to change his perception of Christians.

Amazingly for me, I didn't bite back. I didn't tell him in that moment, *"I'm a Christian."* Instead, I asked him some questions to try to understand what he thought and why. What followed was an hour of him unloading years of annoyance and frustration about how he felt he had been treated by Christians and the church. For Ken, it turned into a bit of a therapy session!

When he had got it all out, he turned to me saying, "You've not said what you believe?" At that point, I said, "I'm a Christian." He stopped in his tracks and said, "I can't believe that! I've been criticising Christianity for an hour and you haven't butted in or defended your beliefs once. You just listened." That conversation – where for once I just took the time to listen and understand – opened the door to Ken wanting to have lots of conversations about life and faith.

Later on, when he had some personal challenges, Ken was quick to chat with me about them and ask for advice. And over time Ken and his wife, daughter and grandson all became part of a local church, with two of them getting baptised.

What's the lesson here? Sometimes as Christians we can feel so pressured to tell others what we think, that we forget to listen – and listening can be the biggest gift we can give someone. Listening shows that I care. It shows that I am interested in what you think. It shows that I value and accept you as a person, regardless of whether your thoughts match up with mine. Listening is one of the most amazing ways of fulfilling Jesus' Great Commandment to *"Love your Neighbour"*, and it can also open up the door for us to be heard in return.

My Mum was the best person I've known at listening. She absolutely would NOT have called herself an evangelist. She hated the thought of standing in the centre of town preaching, or door-knocking to tell people about Jesus, but as I grew up there were huge numbers of people with all sorts of issues who one by one would come and sit at my Mum's kitchen table. Mum would make them a drink, and just listen to them for as long as they needed. She never preached, never criticised, but just valued them to the point of stopping whatever else was going on so she could give them her undivided attention.

It turns out that she was the greatest 'evangelist' my old church has ever seen, but never by preaching. She did it by valuing, loving and listening to people. And then the time would come for so many of those people where they would say, *"What can I do Alison?"* And that question would be the door opening for her to share the love and message of Jesus with them.

It seemed that the more people she loved and listened to, the more people God sent to sit at her kitchen table. At her funeral in 2016, there were around 200 people who affectionately called her *'My second Mum'* or *'Auntie Alison'* and who said that it was her who led them to Jesus.

Do you want people around you to know Jesus in their lives? The great news is that God calls you first to listen to them. Listen to their beliefs, understand their life, find out what makes them tick. Way before he is calling you to preach to people, God is calling you to listen to them! People will experience God's love and care through your listening, and this can lead to them opening the door to hear about the God you believe in.

WHAT ARE THEY ASKING FOR?

When I was first a Christian, I felt that the most important thing was to tell people about Jesus, whether or not they wanted to hear it. I would always be on the lookout for an 'opening' so I could begin a conversation about faith. Now this isn't actually a bad thing in itself; God opens doors for conversations and it's great to be looking for those opportunities.

The problem for me was that, rather than looking for God-given moments, I would try to shoehorn conversations of faith in where the other person really wasn't looking to have them. I would ask someone what they did at the weekend so that they could ask me too. And when they did, **BAM!** That was my opportunity to mention going to church and to give them a debrief of the sermon that was preached. You can imagine that at times this led to the other person feeling pretty uncomfortable!

We once took someone to watch the Lion, the Witch and the Wardrobe at the cinema. The story is an allegory of Jesus dying for us, so surely this was a great opportunity for me to talk about Jesus with them. After the film they talked all about what they thought of it, but they didn't see any connection to Jesus at all. To me this was a great disappointment, so I took it upon myself to start talking about Jesus, which led to them asking me and Tanya to never talk about our faith again… ever! This was not the outcome of the evening I was hoping for.

So what was the issue? What went wrong? I believe the issue was that there is a real difference between God opening up a conversation about Himself by creating spiritual interest in someone, and us trying to ram Jesus into the middle of a conversation.

So let's ask ourselves: Do we value people enough to LISTEN to them? To hear what they are saying? To hear what they are wanting? To hear what they are asking for?

When I ignore what's important to them I diminish their value. I put my own priorities above theirs. What they then feel is, *"You're not really interested in me; you're just interested in your own beliefs,"* or, *"You just want to make me like you."*

Do you and I value someone enough to meet them where they're at, on their terms? It's costly putting others before ourselves, but this is crucial if we're going to fulfil Jesus' call to *"Love our neighbour."*

Spending time having a coffee with someone and just listening to them reveals how we value them. And it reflects something beautiful – that the God we follow is worth considering.

A HELPFUL TIP: TEST THE WATER AND RESPECT THEIR RESPONSE

One thing that I do find helpful sometimes is to just pop something small to do with church or faith into a conversation and listen to the response. If someone changes the subject, that's them saying, *"I don't want to get into this type of conversation."* So feel free to go with their desire to leave it there. But if they respond keenly or begin to ask questions, that's their green light to chat further. If they're not ready to talk about God, you can continue to talk to God about them in prayer, asking Him to lead them to an openness towards Him.

Remember, they're precious and it's their prerogative to have that conversation or not. Unless you feel certain God wants you to nudge further, relax and move on to chatting about something else.

9

COMMON GROUND

"Greater love has no one than this, that someone lay down his life for his friends."

John 15v13

At Welcome Church, for years, we had a Groundsman called Colin. He was a lovely guy who had been part of the church for decades and loved a chat. He'd regularly talk about his daughter Suzi and her husband Dan. Suzi had grown up in the church but hadn't been coming for years. Colin told me how he'd love Dan to come to faith and how he'd love the two of them to bring their girls to church. He mentioned that Dan loves football and golf.

I was introduced to Dan a few weeks later. We chatted, and of course talked football and golf. I invited him to have a game of golf with me and a couple of other guys at a nice course I had access to, which he was quick to accept. Our conversation on the golf course was about the big things in life: whether Fulham were going to get relegated, and whether it was a 6-iron or a 7-iron for the next shot.

Dan's a really nice bloke. We naturally hit it off as we played golf together, and we both enjoyed the game and the beer afterwards. Tanya and I then had Dan and Suzi and their two girls over for lunch one Sunday, and we had a follow-up game of golf with one of my friends from church and one of Dan's friends.

We had common interests: sport and the age of our kids. And we also enjoyed each other's company.

A few months later I invited Dan to attend our Alpha Launch. My pitch was this, *"The comedian looks more like you than you do, so come along and see him!"* Dan agreed, and then asked if he could bring his friend Russell. I put Dan and Russell on Mike and Lou's table, because they're great hosts and Mike would have lots in common with them.

At the end of the evening, when we encouraged people to sign up to Alpha Week 1, both Dan and Russell signed up. To me this was unexpected but amazing! And over the next nine weeks, they shared their doubts, asked their questions, and little by little were warming up to Jesus.

When the Alpha Course finished Mike and Lou's table continued to meet as a Life Group each week. Spiritual momentum was growing and God was revealing Himself to the group bit by bit. Around four months after Alpha finished, Dan had become a Christian and was baptised.

God has given us all interests to enjoy, and he loves it when we enjoy doing them with others. Because He is God and He loves people, in that space of 'doing life' with others through common interests God will work to begin to draw people to Him. What an amazing God! Firstly, to love people enough to draw them to Himself. Secondly, to use us to do it. And thirdly to allow that all to happen as we naturally 'do life' with others, doing things we enjoy doing!

AT THIS POINT, LET'S STOP AND THINK:

Who has God placed in your life that you have a common connection with? Take time to think this through. You could even write some names down.

Next, pause and pray that God would use your relationships with those people to draw them to Himself.

Moving forward, as you spend time with these people, watch for conversations to be instigated by them about life and faith, and just be ready to allow those conversations to happen. Don't be surprised when they do because the God who loves them is at work through you and in them.

Why not get in contact with your friends, neighbours or colleagues and arrange to connect over your common interest soon?

10

MEET A NEED

"I tell you the truth, whatever you did for one of the least of these brothers of mine, you did for me."

Matthew 25v40

If you're a Christian, you'll probably be aware of Jesus' call to care for others. It was something Jesus did throughout His ministry on earth, and something He spoke really clearly about. These verses are part of a section of Jesus' teaching on caring for those in need – feeding the hungry, giving a drink to the thirsty, inviting a stranger in, clothing the naked, looking after the sick, visiting prisoners.

The church throughout the last 2,000 years since Jesus spoke these words has looked to fulfil this high calling in numerous ways: early Christians would care for lepers, take orphans in and look after them as their own, and care for the elderly. Worldwide organisations such as the Red Cross, Christian Aid, Tear Fund, Compassion and many others have been looking after the poor of the world for years and years, whilst Prison Fellowship, the biggest worldwide ministry to prisoners, is a Christian organisation that has been caring for convicts for decades.

Nationally we have amazing charities like Foodbank providing food support and Christians Against Poverty (CAP) helping to alleviate debt and poverty across the UK. Your church is very likely involved in various Social Action ministries to care for people with all sorts of different areas of need.

Regularly meeting a need becomes something that is best done as a small group or as a whole church, but meeting a need always seems to start with one Christian reaching out and meeting one individuals' needs.

And as we read these words of Jesus, *"I tell you the truth, whatever you did for one of the least of these brothers of mine, you did for me,"* (Matthew 25v40), we get a sense of how important, how precious it is to Jesus that His followers follow His example and reach out to support those we see around us.

So, what does our meeting someone's needs do?

Firstly, it honours Jesus as we fulfil His call to care. Jesus tells us we're doing it FOR Him, on His behalf. Secondly, we can be confident as a result that the person will encounter Jesus' compassion and love through us. Thirdly, a Christian meeting someone's real needs is so often the door that God opens for them to become receptive to the message of Jesus. We've considered in chapter 4, "Care Before you Share", how caring opens the door to sharing, how people experiencing our love opens the door to hearing the message of Jesus. Receiving help from you can and regularly will lead to the other person moving from being closed to open towards your faith and the One you follow.

When we see someone in our lives with a need Jesus calls us to reach out, offer support, love, encouragement and where possible, to meet that need; and to do it gladly, freely and without any expectation of anything in return. It's also so important to have in mind that this person's real need, their lack, their struggle, their sickness, ultimately can only be solved by the great doctor, Jesus himself. Over time we're called not just to meet people's needs but to bring those who are sick, hurting or struggling to Jesus, like the men who carried their disabled friend on a mat and lowered him at Jesus' feet.

Now, in post-Christian Britain, most people know next to nothing about Jesus, so when realising they've got a need that they can't solve they aren't all of a sudden saying, *"I realise I need Jesus!"* And that's ok – who Jesus is, what Jesus has done, why Jesus can solve all of our deepest needs are all things that can be revealed over the course of time.

But when someone has a presenting need it can be a starting point; a door that can open a journey towards faith in Jesus. It's so important that our aim is always to point others to Jesus. Perhaps a good way to look at it is this: Jesus is the doctor, we're given the role of triage nurse, to identify the need (with the Holy Spirit's help), and we're possibly the nurse who can bandage people back up, but let's always have in mind that at the right time we want to introduce them to the Great Doctor.

As you look up at the people God has placed all around you, and as your desire to love people towards Jesus is growing, perhaps a starting point is to ask Him, *"Show me those in need you've placed around me? Give me an opening to draw near to them today / this week to support them, and as I do so please enable me over time to point them towards You."*

11

YOU WERE DESIGNED TO SHINE!

*Jesus said, "**I am the light of the world**.
Whoever follows me will never walk in darkness,
but will have the light of life"
John 8v12*

*Jesus said, "**You are the light of the world**.
A city on a hill cannot be hidden.
Neither do people light a lamp and put it under a bowl.
Instead they put it on its stand, and it gives light to everyone in the house.
In the same way, let your light shine before men,
that they may see your good deeds and glorify your Father in heaven."
Matthew 5v14-16*

I find Jesus' claim that HE is the light of the world easy to accept. When He walked the earth, people were drawn to Him like moths around a flame: from 'religious' people like Nicodemus the Pharisee through to 'sinful' tax collectors and prostitutes, as well as 'down-and-out's' who were desperate for hope. Individuals visited Him at night, and huge crowds flocked around Him by day. His miracles transformed lives, and His teaching transformed hearts. Jesus' disciple Peter summed up what people were experiencing when he said to Him, *"You have the words to eternal life"* (John 6v68). And Jesus' impact on planet earth ever since then has been to shine brightly as He has personally drawn a few billion people to Him. I personally am one of these people – my life and my heart affected eternally by Him.

So when Jesus claims He is the light of the world, my response is simple: *"Yes Jesus, you definitely are!"*

But His suggestion that I have become the light of the world??? That feels much harder to accept. Erm … awkward. Sorry Jesus, I think you've got the wrong person; there's absolutely no comparison, there's no light shining here I'm afraid.

What about you; do you believe Jesus when He says YOU are the light of the world?

So many Christians simply don't believe this is true of them – they don't see themselves as a light that reflects Jesus. Perhaps the issue is that we can so often be aware of our own failings that we can write ourselves off. *"No not me, Jesus. I'm no shining light. Perhaps Mother Theresa but not me."*

But if we choose NOT to believe Jesus here, what are we saying? Is Jesus lying; or perhaps just mistaken? Really? As we think this through, how can we possibly say Jesus, the Son of God, the perfect one, the sinless one, the only wise one, is a liar or a fool? We don't think that about Him at all, do we?

So while it may feel like humility saying, *"That's not me – I'm NOT the light of the world,"* I've come to realise that it's not humility at all – it's actually a lack of faith in the work Jesus has done in us. Just as we met Jesus as sinners and were saved by His grace, so we were in darkness and have been transformed by His light to us and then through us. We didn't save ourselves; it was all the work of Jesus. So too, we didn't make ourselves light, it was Jesus, the Light of the World, pouring his light into us.

Believing *"I am the light of the world"* is in no way arrogant. It's faith – believing that our amazing Saviour has not just saved us but has also done what He promises here and poured His light into us that will shine through us as we interact with others.

What if you and I chose to believe Jesus' claims about us, that He has poured His light into us? It would fundamentally affect how we live our lives and what we expect from our interactions with everyone we meet, wouldn't it?

REFLECTING JESUS' LIGHT

Let me give you a slightly different analogy to further underline the impact of Jesus' light on us.

The sun shines so brightly that we can't look directly at it. If we did, we would be blinded by it. The sun has an incredible impact on everything in its path: grass grows, plants bud and flower, fruit changes colour. It even has the strength to warm the oceans.

The moon on the other hand has no light coming from within it, yet at night the moon shines brightly and can even light up the night sky. Although the moon has no light coming from within itself, the sun's rays are so bright that the moon reflects those rays and it shines brightly too. That's a small picture of what God does with us.

Revelation 1 describes Jesus' face as *"like the sun shining in all of its brilliance."* And EVERY CHRISTIAN (yes, I've put it in caps to highlight this includes you and me) is like the moon, we shine because we reflect the brightness of Jesus, the Son.

There is a huge difference, however. The moon receives its light from a great distance and is just a pale reflection of the brightness of the sun, reflecting between 3% and 12% of the suns power. By contrast, we reflect Jesus' light not from a distance, but because God has placed the same Holy Spirit in us that He placed in Jesus!

2 Corinthians 3v18 tells us, *"We with unveiled faces all reflect the Lord's glory."* It's not an overstatement to say that you and I can shine as brightly today as Jesus did when he walked the earth.

HAVING AN IMPACT

A lack of belief that Jesus has now made US the light of the world will affect how we live and interact with others. We can have the brightness and power of Jesus' Spirit within us but not believe it and instead hide it, like putting a lamp under a bowl. The light of Jesus in us has such potential to bring warmth, goodness and blessing to people all around us, but hidden under a bowl no-one will see it and no-one will experience the benefit of it.

Over the last few months Jesus has been stirring me to believe that I really am the light of the world. Not in an arrogant way, as I've said – this is not about puffing ourselves up to try to look good. In fact, the Bible reminds us in 2 Corinthians 4v7 that *"we have this treasure in jars of clay to show that this all-surpassing power is from God and not from us."* I am simply learning to believe that what Jesus has said about me is true: that He's put His Spirit in me, which will cause Him to shine brightly through me. I can go about my business, bumping into whoever comes across my path, and they will encounter something of Jesus' goodness along the way.

What an empowering thing to believe. And what a difference it makes to my faith and expectation levels as I live my life! I am the light of the world because I'm radiating Jesus' light that lives in me. People will be blessed by God when they interact with me. Amazing!

So, as we let our light shine, what impact should we expect to have on people all around us? As Jesus explains, *"... that they may see your good deeds and glorify your Father in heaven."* People will experience something Heavenly through Jesus' light permeating out of you and me, through our actions of kindness and love, and it will lead to lots of people opening up to the One who put the light into us!

Corinne has been coming to our Friday lunch – Welcome Meal – for over 20 years. When she was feeling down because of circumstances in her life, a couple of people from the team prayed for her. This then led to the beginning of a journey for her, to Alpha and eventually to attending church on a Sunday. Over the course of time, she was baptised having placed her faith in Jesus. Amazing!

Corinne told me during that time that her 70th birthday was coming up, and that John and Sheila, an amazing couple from Welcome Church who reached out and welcomed Corinne into their lives, were putting on a birthday party for her. This is a lovely gesture, and it's even more precious than you're imagining. *Corinne told me this was the first birthday party anyone had put on for her since she became an adult.* What an incredible example of Jesus' love shining through his people to make a huge impact in someone else's life!

Wenxing and Yan Li moved to Woking from Beijing, China at the beginning of 2016. Wenxing was going to start a business here. After three months not one other person in Woking had even spoken to them. Life was lonely.

They then bumped into Meg from Welcome Church in a local park. Meg began a conversation with them. From this interaction, Meg invited Yan and her youngest son to Welcome Tots, a toddler group held at Welcome Church each week. Yan loved it. Her son had lots of fun and she was beginning to meet new friends. Loneliness was being replaced by relationship.

The family then happened to walk past the Welcome Centre one Sunday morning as we were hosting a 'Welcome Kids' Sunday event alongside a breakfast for parents. They were invited in, met some friendly people who cared for them, and enjoyed community. This moment was hugely impactful, especially for Wenxing. Before they arrived in the UK they had heard of Jesus and assumed He was 'the God of Europe'. They were now beginning to encounter His love for themselves through His followers.

They then decided they wanted to come to church on a Sunday to understand more about Jesus. Although they couldn't understand the words being sung, both describe themselves experiencing deep emotions during the worship times. Yan would have tears flowing down her face week after week as God's loves was touching her heart. I remember the morning when Marion brought them across to the Communion table. She said to me, *"Yan and Wenxing are going to take Communion for the first time today, because they've both decided to become Christians."*

In that moment, I found tears rolling down my own cheeks as I was blown away by the work of God in their lives. The testimonies they gave as they were baptised, helped by someone from Welcome Church who spoke Mandarin, reduced most of the room to tears. What began with a Christian saying hello at a local park, led on to a community that offered friendship. This led to their spiritual interest being sparked and resulted in the God of love who was behind it all revealing Himself to this couple in such a deep and rich way that they decided to give their lives to Jesus! It all began with a Christian who stepped out and let Jesus shine through her.

PAUSE TO PRAY

Do you want Jesus to have an impact on people in your life? If so, let me encourage you to begin by praying, "Jesus I choose to believe that you have made me the light of the world, and that people will be impacted by you through me. Help me to shine brightly for you, that people in my life would turn to you."

12

YOU'RE GOD'S GIFT!

"The Spirit of the Sovereign LORD is on me, because the LORD has anointed me to preach good news to the poor, He has sent me to bind up the broken-hearted, to proclaim freedom for the captives and release from darkness for the prisoners, to proclaim the year of the LORD's favour..."

Isaiah 61v1-2

I remember when Nathan's fiancée came to a staff Christmas party. Jules is from America, she'd flown in that morning, and it was the first time many of us had met her. They spent most of the day making desserts for the party, turning up with 4 big and delicious looking cakes!

When it came to pudding time, we all tried at least 2 cakes each. And wow! They really were pretty special!

"Jules, these puddings are AMAZING!!" I called out to her across the party. *"Yes, they are."* she replied, simply and matter-of-factly.

The reality was, they were spectacular, and they were a lovely and gratefully received gift. And Jules agreeing was simply her being truthful. In fact, it would have been weird and untruthful if she'd said anything other. But it felt quite an unusual comment for someone to make. Here in Britain, being self-deprecating is almost seen as a quality. *"I'm rubbish!" "It's a bit too sweet actually," "Ahh, I guess it's ok."* These are the sorts of comments a British person may make when a compliment is paid.

One of the problems with this is we refuse to see what others see. And as a Christian, if we're not careful we can refuse to see what God sees in us. *"I'm a loser!" "I'm a sinner!" "God would never use me!"* These are just some of the things we may be saying to ourselves – and according to God they're just not true.

When you place your faith in Jesus, 2 Corinthians 5v17 reminds us that you are now *"in Christ... a new creation – the old has gone, the new has come!"* You're no longer a loser, no longer the person you were. And you start becoming a little more like Christ each day.

As you interact with other people, what do they experience? Well, as you get to know Jesus and start to experience Him more in your life, others start to experience Him THROUGH YOU too! You've got good news to share – the best news. And more than that, you ARE good news – people will be blessed by being with you! What an incredible gift you've become to people all around you – you have become their meeting place with God!

I heard one of Neil's family members was seriously ill in hospital, so I wanted to reach out. We knew each other but weren't close up to that point, had never hung out as friends, but I just felt stirred to get in touch. We met, we walked, and we chatted. I wanted to offer support – and I also wanted to see if God wanted to work through me to draw Neil back to Him. Neil had left church as a teenager over 20 years ago, but the worry about a loved one's illness was causing him to look for help and hope. As we chatted our conversations quickly led to speaking about God, speaking about peace, and speaking about praying for healing. Just being around a Christian was all Neil seemed to need to begin re-connecting with God in this time of worry after all those years.

When I meet up with people, I tend to just pop things about my faith or my church into conversations, to see where they are at and how they respond. If someone ignores it or swerves it, we'll move on – I'll take it as a sign that God isn't stirring them at that moment in time. But if they respond and ask questions, I'll take that as a small opening of a door, a sign that God may be at work, and allow that conversation to continue.

As I met with Neil, I wanted to see if he was open to deeper conversations about faith. After our second meet-up, I asked him as we came to the end of our walk, *"Is there anything I can do to support or help you through this?"* *"Well, you mentioned Alpha – I think that may be good for me,"* Neil replied. And that was that – he signed up for Alpha that day and joined in with the next session the following week.

When I was a teenager, I was convinced I was "God's gift" to everyone female. At parties, I was sure that all the girls fancied me. When I walked down the road with friends, if there was a girl walking past us, I would regularly tell my friends, *"She was looking at me!"* I think the term for what was going on is 'delusional.'

And yet although I really wasn't God's gift back then, 25 years later the Bible has convinced me that NOW I am God's gift – but you'll be pleased to hear not in the ways I used to think! The verses above from Isaiah help me understand this: *"The Spirit of the Sovereign LORD is on me, because the LORD has anointed me to preach good news to the poor, He has sent me to bind up the broken-hearted, to proclaim freedom for the captives and release from darkness for the prisoners, to proclaim the year of the LORD's favour...".* Jesus, 700 years after Isaiah wrote these prophetic words, told us that He was the fulfilment of this promise. After reading those words from Isaiah in the temple, Jesus went on to say, *"Today this scripture is fulfilled in your hearing."* (Luke 4v21).

Just as Jesus was God's gift to the world when He walked the earth 2,000 years ago, so He has now made you and me God's gift to people all around us by putting the same Holy Spirit in us. Now, clearly, there are some big differences: Jesus is God's perfect one and only Son, whereas we've been adopted into his family. Jesus was begotten, we are created. Jesus was perfect, we are forgiven sinners being made perfect by him. Jesus is the Saviour, we have been saved by him.

However, we're not suffering from a Messiah Complex when we say *"I am God's gift"* – we're just believing Jesus' words over us. When Jesus returned to heaven, He empowered his followers by the Holy Spirit to do *"greater things"* than He did. You and I have become the place where God dwells, and as a result people are blessed to be around us!

Having confidence that God is at work, and specifically having confidence that God is at work THROUGH YOU is such an empowering truth to remember. When you meet someone, they're encountering the presence of God in you. It's no exaggeration to say that **God loves people so much that He's placed you in their lives**!

As you take time to reach out in love to someone, they can experience the compassion of Jesus through you. As you connect with someone who is struggling or hurting, they can experience the peace and strength of God through you. And as you pray for someone, they can experience the healing of God through your prayers.

We're not losers. We're not an inconvenience. We're not like an irritating fly that someone wants to swat! The truth according to God is SO DIFFERENT to all of that. According to the Bible, you and I are **God's gift** to the people He's placed around us – they'll be blessed as they interact with us, they'll experience the love of God through us, and they'll be drawn to Jesus as a result!

13

PATIENCE = PERSEVERANCE

The Lord is not slow in keeping His promise, as some understand slowness. He is patient with you, not wanting anyone to perish, but everyone to come to repentance.

2 Peter 3v9

What does patience look like from God's perspective?

Why does God show patience towards humanity – what's his purpose behind it? Why does He persist in showing patience with us when we all instinctively want to do things our own way, want to play god in our own lives rather than allow him to be God over us?

The verses above show us the simple answer – God has an unwavering desire to see everyone come to repentance – to come to Him and to receive forgiveness through Jesus.[4] Because of His love and grace for us, God is playing the long game with humankind.

If you're a Christian, I'm sure you're eternally grateful for God's patience towards you. None of us were born good, none of us were born a Christian. Romans 3v23 reminds us, *"all have sinned and fallen short of the glory of God."* Every single one of us NEEDED SAVING, and God's patience towards us meant we were given opportunity after opportunity to come to him, and when we did, we experienced the kindness and patience of a loving Father, just as

---

[4] I'm not intending to open up the 'Calvinist' vs 'Arminian' debate here!

Jesus promised we would when He told the parable of the Prodigal son.

We ALL have benefitted from the long-suffering patience that God has shown to us! For me, growing up in a Christian household, the son of parents who loved Jesus, the grandson of a Missionary; I had hundreds of opportunities to receive Jesus from a young age. And yet, I walked away from church aged 16 and was 25 when I eventually came to faith. How did God deal with me throughout that time? With gentleness, with perseverance and with patience. And that's how He's dealt with you.

If that's how God has behaved towards us, how should we expect him to behave towards others around us who haven't yet come to Jesus? The good news is God doesn't deal with them how **we** might sometimes want to – with frustration, ready to give up on them! The answer is obvious when you think about it: **God shows patience to those around us too, just as He has to us.** He is the patient God – that is His character; that is who He is. And the reason given here for God's patience is that He doesn't want anyone to perish – to die distant from Him, without Christ; in contrast He desires that everyone would come to repentance, to accept Jesus' death for them, to receive forgiveness, to be made a new creation in Christ, to be brought into God's family, to be given a future and an eternal hope in Him!

That's God's desire, that's His reason for showing such enduring, long-suffering patience towards us AND those around us.

As we reflect on God's patience, what can we learn from Him in how we should deal with those around us, specifically those who haven't yet come to Jesus? Well surely God desires that we should reflect Him, to share His desire that our loved ones would come to faith in Jesus, and as a result to endure in patience towards them even if it's been YEARS and they still seem far off from Him.

So what are the characteristics of God's patience that we can show to others?

Firstly, we come back to love. Love is God's motivation for His patience. He created every human being in love, it's His love that means He desires we would all come to repentance, and it's His love that is leading Him to show patience towards us all as we stumble, pause or go backwards on our journeys towards Him. Our love for God and others needs to be the primary reason we should be showing patience towards others in our lives.

Secondly, perseverance – to not give up. If someone has rejected God's offer of forgiveness 20 years ago, God perseveres, God shows patience – He looks to give another opportunity for them to hear about and to receive Jesus. We know this patience in our own lives, and this verse written by Peter helps us KNOW this patience is being shown to others too.

So, as we begin to think of people in and around our lives – our loved ones who have walked away from faith, our friends who have turned their noses up at our faith, our work colleagues who have changed the subject when we mention our faith, it's so important that we remember HOW God is dealing with them - patiently, and WHY He is dealing with them like this – because He wants to give further opportunities for them to place their faith in His Son.

What does that mean? It means that a 'No' yesterday isn't necessarily a 'No' forever. And a rejected invitation to Alpha or church doesn't mean we can never make a second, third or even tenth invite. I remember when Becky filmed her "Welcome Story"[5] she said her mum invited her to Alpha "for the millionth time," and she eventually said 'Yes'. Note – there may be a touch of hyperbole in Becky's comment, but the fact remained her mum so desired Becky to meet Jesus that she patiently invited her to Alpha again and again. And again. And again.

From the early days of Tanya and me becoming Christians, her brother Clint wasn't at all interested. He described himself as a 'sceptical agnostic' and felt science had all but disproved God. We learnt pretty quickly that it was a topic to tread carefully around with him.

And yet, we had a real desire that Clint would come to experience Jesus for himself, knowing the love and transformation Jesus provides. But what could we do? It felt as though the door was well and truly closed!

We were so excited when we heard Clint and his fiancé Magda were moving to Woking a couple of years ago. It meant our family could see them more regularly, which was great. Clint's that dream Uncle, full of energy and fun with the kids! It also meant we had an easier invite we could make to church at the right time, which was now just up the road. And so, as our church approached the opening of our new building, we made an invite for them to join us. Clint & Magda agreed to come, as did lots of other friends. We were excited that they were there, and nervous about how they'd find it.

They loved it – finding it really uplifting, walking out afterwards feeling energised and inspired. They agreed to come again. And

---

[5] Welcome Stories are videos of people from Welcome Church sharing their story of God's impact on their lives. See www.welcomestories.uk

again. And when Alpha started a few weeks later, they said yes to that too.

We recently filmed Clint's Alpha Story where he said that he'd gone "from zero interest in Christianity and God to doing Alpha, realising afterwards that it was the start of a new, ongoing spiritual journey" for him. Can you imagine how excited we are?!

Oh, did I mention: the time lag between us becoming Christians and Clint beginning his spiritual journey was a small matter of 18 years!

What can we all learn from Clint's story when we put it alongside 2 Peter 3v9? We can learn that God continues to be patient with people because of His great love and desire for them to come to Him, and we can learn that a previous 'No' doesn't mean a 'No' forever. As we patiently persevere in loving and inviting, God turns yesterday's no's into yes's today, He turns agnostics into explorers, and He turns scepticism into faith, as He gently draws people to Himself!

As we consider these things, let's not write off people who may have previously rejected our invites. If you've got friends or loved ones who have walked away from, or rejected faith, allow Clint's story and the truth in this verse about God's patient perseverance towards them encourage you to continue to pray, to persevere, and to invite.

14

LOOK UP!

"Look, I tell you, LIFT UP YOUR EYES, and see that the fields are ripe for harvest."

John 4v35 (ESV)

There's about 20 different 'Vic-isms' in our family – phrases that my Dad (Vic) would regularly say, such as *"Worse things happen at sea,"* when one of his grandchildren cuts their knee. One of the phrases he's been known to say is, *"There's none so blind as those who don't want to see!"*

This is a really great phrase when it comes to thinking about our attitude towards making invites to a church event, to Alpha or to church on a Sunday. *"No-one in my life would want to come,"* can be the knee-jerk response so many Christians can have.

So – an honesty moment. Is this actually true? Is there literally no-one we could make that invite to? Is there no-one in our lives interested in our faith or our invites? Or do we perhaps suffer from selective blindness – CHOOSING NOT TO SEE the people in our lives who we can invite?

Let me encourage you to really think deeply about your answer to this, and to tell God about your feelings. After all, God knows our thoughts before He hears our prayers – He already knows what's behind us not making those invites. Is it easier to write everyone off around us as "not interested," rather than look up – for people we can make those invites to and expose ourselves to the possible awkwardness or disappointment of a rejected invite?

What if the opposite was actually true? What if there were people literally ALL AROUND US who COULD say 'Yes' to that invite, who WOULD be interested in finding out more about the faith that has transformed us? What if some people are interested deep-down but just don't know it yet, whereas others are literally waiting for us to just connect and invite them?

Well, according to Jesus in John 4v35, there are many people who are interested – positioned by Him and ready to begin that journey of faith that will lead to Him! How would Jesus respond to our comments of *"No-one's interested"*? He'd say to us, *"Look, I tell you, lift up your eyes and see that the fields are ripe for harvest."* (John 4v35).

Let's remember the backdrop of that sentence. Jesus was with His disciples on the outskirts of a Samaritan village – the "faithless enemy" according to many with Jesus that day. The disciples were on the fringe of what they felt was a desolate place for faith; Jesus saw it as a place where faith was about to burst into life!

The other side of this story is also worth considering. Jesus has just had a deep conversation at a well with a sad, lonely woman who had been shunned by her society. She knew what it was like to be rejected, and so was taken aback by Jesus' care and conversation. After chatting to her for a while, Jesus revealed who He was – the Messiah everyone had been waiting for. He was the hope she was looking for to receive acceptance and forgiveness.

The woman was shocked, stunned! And what did she do with this news? Did she keep it to herself? Did she not tell anyone in her village because she knew they hated her? Did she stay silent because she was convinced no-one would want to listen? Did she keep schtum because she wasn't wise enough to explain everything theologically? No! She rushed back into her village and made a life-changing invite! *"Come and see!"* was her simple encouragement (John 4v29). This wasn't a wise theologian who had finally qualified to evangelise her town after decades of study. This was simply a woman who had been transformed by an encounter with Jesus who then invited people to investigate for themselves. *"Come and see!"*, is something we can all say, isn't it?

So, what happened next? How did the people in this woman's village respond to her invite? What did Jesus' disciples see as they lifted their eyes? A huge crowd of people were being brought to Jesus, led by this Samaritan woman! John chapter 4 continues with us discovering that *"many of the Samaritans from that town believed in Him."* (John 4v39).

The disciples had a big shock that would've redefined their expectations of Jesus' power to save as they lifted their eyes from their conversation they looked up and saw loads of people walking out of that village to come to meet Jesus! An unlikely Samaritan town was experiencing revival because one woman's invite coincided with Jesus' desire to save people! Jesus knows where He's planting small seeds of faith, and He knows when He's going to pour water on those seeds and see them sprout into life.

Do you and I want to see people around us come to faith? There are three simple things Jesus wants these words of His to stir us to do. Firstly, BELIEVE JESUS as He makes these statements about people all around us being like crops in fields that are *"ripe for harvest"*. Secondly, simply LOOK UP, lift our eyes above our busyness, away from our 'to do' lists, to see those He's placed around us. And thirdly, to REACH OUT, believing He's at work.

During lockdown, Tanya and I were outside Ethan's nursery one morning when we saw a dad from the school gate. I'd seen him around, but we didn't know each other very well. I smiled and said, "Hi." This led to a conversation, which led to him asking what I do, which in turn led to me mentioning, among other things, Alpha. *"I've heard of Alpha, and thought I'd like to do it at some point,"* said Darren to my great surprise. A couple of months later, a few days before I'm writing this chapter, Darren signed up to join us for Alpha Online next week!

Maybe that's just a fluke. Maybe it's just Dub's luck and maybe you're not that lucky when it comes to faith conversations and Alpha invites. Or maybe it's the reality of looking up to see what Jesus promised to me today in Woking, 2,000 years ago as he stood outside a dusty, hot Samaritan village – fields of people all around us that He plans to draw to Himself through our connections and our invites.

I've placed this chapter, *"Look up!"*, where God seems to draw people towards Him in a moment, alongside the *"Patience = Perseverance"* chapter as they sit alongside each other in such an interesting way – the seemingly momentary alongside the lifelong. One thing remains true over it all – Jesus' words that, "*My Father is always at his work to this very day, and I too am working."* (John 5v17). We can't always see it, at times we don't even recognise it, but we can be **CONFIDENT** that God has been working in the lives of so many people around us before we even connect with them. What an important thing to remember – reminding us that we don't need to try to create something out of nothing, more that we can step in to what God is already doing as we decide to stop, look up and reach out to others.

As we draw this chapter to a close, a question: Can we *really know* there are people around us and in our lives who we can see come to faith in Jesus? The answer is Yes we can: He's placed them there, as we'll see in the next chapter!

15

PLACED THERE BY GOD!

God determined the times set for them and the exact places where they should live. God did this so that men would seek Him and perhaps reach out for Him and find Him, though He is not far from each one of us.

Acts 17v26-27

The above verses are worth reading again. And again.

Where I live is not an accident. Right alongside Tanya and I making our decision about where we were going to live, the God who created us chose WHEN we'd be born and how long we'd live for, AND WHERE we would live! There's no accident in our current location – it has been pre-planned by God himself!

The same is true for you too. God has determined the times set for YOU (WHEN) and the exact place WHERE you live. Feel free to read Acts 17v26 again and allow it to sink in a little more. Your timeline and your location are God's plan!

The same is also true for my neighbours and yours, my work colleagues and yours, those who you and I share hobbies with, those who are the parents of our kids' friends – everyone we come into contact with has been placed around us by God.

You're getting the point – and it's a huge, mind-blowing one. God is Sovereign – He's in control. And God has a plan behind your and my location, as well as everyone whose lives are connected to ours. He decided which people would live, work and spend their free time around YOU.

Wow!

It reminds me a little of "The Truman Show," a fascinating Jim Carrey movie where without knowing it Truman has been placed into a huge movie set in the form of a fake town, and the director orchestrates every interaction Truman will make each day. The director chose who Truman would marry, who his friends would be, who his neighbours would be, which company would give him a job, even which person would sell him his daily newspaper. One day, it's as though the lightbulb goes on, and it begins to dawn on Truman that he's being watched.

The director in the Truman Show didn't want Truman to know his meetings and conversations were planned, or that his life was there as viewing fodder for the watching millions, so he worked hard to try to cover this up and keep Truman believing there was nothing unusual about his seemingly mundane life.

There are some similarities and some big differences from The Truman Show to our lives. It's really important to note that the control the movie director tried to have over Truman is completely different to the freedom and choices God has given us! God is not a control-freak, trying to micro-manage every small detail of our lives. The freewill God has given us is real – we have autonomy to make choices, to do our own thing and to go outside of His will for our lives.

But there's a huge amount of planning and coordinating that God has done in our lives, as the verses above show us. God DOES want us to realise the 'movie' He's written us into and to realise the significance of the life He's given us. There is an overarching script

God has written over your life, including details of who lives in your street, who works in your office, who trains at your gym, who is a parent on the schoolgate, and so on. God has planned all of these things ON PURPOSE and FOR A PURPOSE. So why has God gone to these lengths? Why has he decided who we would work, rest and play next to? The answer to this is quite incredible – God wants to take us on a faith adventure to change the lives and the eternal destinations of the people all around us. Just read Acts 17v27:

"God did this so that men would seek him and perhaps reach out for him and find him, though he is not far from each one of us."

There are lots of people in and around my life (let's call it my 'sphere of influence'). And this is down to God's desire that they would reach out for him and find him. Simply put, God has placed specific people around you and me because of His LOVE for them, and His DESIRE to draw them to Him THROUGH US.

So, we can be confident that as we look up (see the previous chapter) and reach out to people all around us, we can and will see some people drawn to God through us. Now there are lots of ways we can reach out badly and lots of ways we can do this well – Part 3 of this book will help us to think these things through. But to have a starting point of, *"God has placed people around me on purpose, so that some will reach out to Him and find Him through me,"* is an amazing starting point of confidence in God being at work BEFORE WE EVEN SAY HI!

God has gone before us and positioned people around us, and then calls us to GO OUT to them and love them towards Jesus.

A few decisions need to be made. How will I prioritise my time? Will I create margin in my life so that I can stop and connect today with that person that God has placed in my path? When I see someone in or around my life hurting or grieving, will I make time to chat, offer an arm round the shoulder, a cuppa or a meal?

Tanya had one of our old friends Hayley due to come and see her one morning, and I had lots of work to do! My plan was to briefly say Hi, to get some work done and to then have half an hour chatting with them a little later. However, as she arrived some big conversations began, and I ended up sitting with them for around an hour and a half. And did I mention I had lots of work to do?!

As our conversations unfolded, I saw how God had planned this catch-up. Our chat led to us discussing how Alpha would be really helpful for her, which she agreed to. She joined us for Alpha session 2 the following week.

Because of Acts 17v26-27 and my own experience bearing this out, my confidence in God orchestrating 'chance meetings' with the right people at the right time continues to grow. And as my confidence grows, the number of significant conversations that lead to invites that then lead to faith in Jesus is growing too.

A MISSIONARY NO LONGER NEEDS TO CROSS THE SEA. A MISSIONARY JUST NEEDS TO CROSS THE ROAD!

It used to be thought that a Missionary was someone who crosses the sea. After all Britain was a 'Christian nation', so the missionaries would go abroad. My Grandpa was a Missionary who sailed to Argentina and spent over 30 years building life with and sharing the gospel with the Wichi, a South American Indian Tribe.

As we reflect on these life-changing verses from the book of Acts, in 21st Century *post-Christian* Britain a Missionary does not need to cross the sea. A Missionary just needs to cross the road to the people God has placed there ready and waiting for us. The UK is a mission field of people God wants to reach through us.

As we go, as we cross the road, the playground or the office with love and kindness to the people God has placed around us, we'll begin to see more and more opportunities to share our lives, to share an invite and, over the course of time to share our faith.

Will you allow God to use Acts 17v26-27 to build your confidence in Him and His plans for the people He's placed around you? What difference can these verses make in your day as you interact with these people God has intentionally positioned you alongside? What difference could these verses make as you consider whether there are people around you that you could connect with, begin to do life with, and invite to Alpha or to church on a Sunday?

WHAT NEXT?

If I were to sum up this whole section, *"Caring – Loving people towards Jesus"*, I would simply say this: my desire was to help you to decide to take Jesus at His word as we considered a wide range of His promises from the Bible – that He wants to win people all around you to him; that He wants to use you in the process; and as you come to trust Jesus in this, that you would be inspired by Him to go and 'do life' with the people He has placed around you, expecting them to be blessed and impacted by God as He draws them to Himself through you.

Someone spending time with you may well be their first step on a journey towards faith. We'll consider what this journey looks like and what other steps we can help them to take in the next section, Step by Step – Loving People on Purpose.

QUESTIONS

What chapters in this section most stood out to you? What surprised you most? In what ways did God most speak to you?

How has this section changed how you view yourself? How has it changed how you view your interactions with others?

How has this section changed your understanding of God's plans for the people He's placed in and around your life?

Who are the people you're going to reach out to and connect with this week? Write them down, pause and pray for them. And then get in touch with them!

PART 3

STEP BY STEP – LOVING PEOPLE ON PURPOSE

We've considered a lot in the previous section about Jesus' call on us to love people towards Him, and we've considered how Jesus plans to use US to reach out to others and love them towards Him. I hope you're finding your confidence in Jesus' desire to use you has massively grown as you've read Part 2 through!

We've got a destination we would love the people in our lives to arrive at – encountering Jesus. So, what's the journey plan? How can they go from where they are today to becoming open to the gospel and receiving Jesus for themselves?

This section, Step by Step, is about looking at how we can now love people on purpose, how we can help them go from where they are today – having a Christian friend who is doing them good (you!) – to ultimately meeting Jesus and receiving all He has for them.

16

LOVING PEOPLE ON PURPOSE!

God does not just sweep life away; instead, He devises ways to bring us back when we have been separated from him.

2 Samuel 14v14

Let's be real about it: God is strategic! God doesn't just flounder around, helpless and hopeless, just wishing people would come to Him. No, He's strategic! He really is. He STRATEGICALLY sent Jesus into the world. He was strategic about WHEN Jesus came. He was strategic about WHY Jesus came – to save the world from our sins and win us back to God. He was strategic about HOW the gospel would go from Jesus to twelve disciples, to 120 followers, to 3,000 people on the day of Pentecost, and then out to the rest of the world.

When Jesus sent out the twelve to preach the good news about Him, He said they should be *"as shrewd as snakes and as innocent as doves";* He wanted them to be strategic about their interactions with everyone.

God was strategic when He saved Saul (later called Paul), and then sent him out across the known world to strategically reach cities and nations with the message of Jesus. And Paul explained something of *his* strategy to do whatever it took to lead people to Christ saying, *"I have become all things to all people so that by all possible means I might save some,"* (1 Corinthians 9v22).

I'm sure you'll agree that none of the verses here show a lack of faith! To state the obvious, Jesus wasn't lacking confidence in God's ability to save people when He told his disciples to be shrewd – He knew they'd face opposition and wanted them to be strategic in how they went. And Paul went on to see thousands and thousands of people come to faith in Jesus because he combined his confidence in Jesus' saving power with a plan for how he was going to approach everyone differently, strategically.

Are you disappointed that you're not seeing people around you come to faith in Jesus? Is your faith in Jesus' saving power waning due to disappointments? Do you feel you had given up hope of seeing loved ones come to Jesus? If so, is it possible that you need to both re-believe Jesus that He has a huge desire to save people in your life AND put a plan in place to, over the course of time, place lots of people in front of Him.

Perhaps even in the spiritual task of leading people to Jesus step-by-step, the old adage proves true that *"if we fail to plan, we're planning to fail."*

Strategy isn't the antithesis of faith. Being strategic about helping those in our lives to take steps towards Jesus isn't us showing a lack of faith in God; it isn't us relying on our own strength; it isn't about believing we can achieve anything without God. The opposite is actually true! Our confidence in the Holy Spirit's power to draw people to Jesus can and should lead us to being like Paul and to create a strategy to put as many people in front of Him as possible!

The friends of the crippled man on a mat knew they couldn't heal him, but had such a huge desire to place him at Jesus' feet that they created a plan, climbed onto a roof, cut a hole and lowered him down right in front of Jesus! Their faith in Jesus led to all of this effort – and they saw their friend healed and saved as a result (Luke 5v17-39).

So, do you have a plan to help take people in your life from where they are now to a place where they're open to hearing the gospel? If not, perhaps I can help you create one. That's what this section of the book, "Step by Step – Loving People On Purpose," is about.

It's important to re-state the (perhaps obvious) motivation for us putting a strategy in place and the clue is in this chapter title – Loving people on purpose. Yes, it's love! But let's consider for a moment the concept of loving people and NOT desiring they come to encounter Jesus for themselves. According to the Bible, a relationship with God through Jesus is the REASON we're on this planet, it's the source of all inner peace, it's the only thing that will transform us from the inside out, it's the only guaranteed ongoing relationship through this life, and it's our only hope for eternity!

In light of these truths, that I'm sure we all hold to, how can it make sense for us to love people and NOT desire for them to come to Jesus? When you really think about it, isn't that actually a weird, perhaps warped, form of love? In fact, is love even the right word for it if we don't desire for people to come to Jesus, the One who has transformed us, the One who is the source of love?

The danger of writing these words is the feelings of heaviness you may feel as you read them. This is NOT aimed at guilting us into sharing our faith or condemning us for every lost opportunity to share Him. Jesus *"came from the Father full of grace and truth"* (John 1v14), and Jesus wants to pour His grace over you in the area of loving people towards Him. But he also wants to graciously speak truth to us in this area, to challenge any sense of "I'll just love people and won't aim to bring them to Jesus." Intellectually and spiritually this position doesn't make sense in the light of Jesus' call on us to go and make disciples, as well as Jesus' absolute significance over every single person's life today and for all eternity. The only thing that makes sense is to desire for people to come to Him, to ask Him to draw them to Him, and to then aim to bring them to Him.

Our love for Jesus and our gratitude for all He's done in our lives, alongside our desire that others would encounter Him as we have, are key motivating factors for looking to draw people to Him. As we think these things through, Jesus is providing us with all of the motivation we need to always be looking for ways to draw people to Him. We can see God's motivation of love as He devises ways so that a lost person may not remain separated from Him – and we can allow God's motivation to be ours as we start to create some plans to love people on purpose, towards Jesus.

The Gospel is the power of God, but the reality is most people in our lives are not ready or open to hearing this gospel – yet. And that's where us creating a plan is so important to help them remove their preconceptions and lower their barriers step by step, until that incredible day that's coming when the gospel is heard and received by them!

"But how do I do that?", I hear you ask. It's all about helping them step by step…

STEP BY STEP

A great question to have in mind when thinking about and praying about them coming to Jesus is, "What is the best next step for them?" Where are they at now? Is there a next step that will help them move a little closer to becoming open to hearing the message of Jesus? I find a great picture to have in mind is one of a 'journey towards faith.'

Just as the old Chinese proverb says that a journey of a thousand miles starts with one small step, regularly those in our lives need to take many small steps before they come to a place of openness to the message of Jesus. And God will give us the ability to help move people from one step to the next as we understand where they're at and think through how they could move a step forward.

It's worth crucially mentioning that many times God can and does work at a much quicker speed – reminding us of John chapter 4v35 where Jesus tells us, *"Do you not say, 'Four months more and then the harvest'? I tell you, open your eyes and look at the fields! They are ripe for harvest."* It's not ALL about strategy and timelines – the Holy Spirit brings people to Jesus in a moment!

However, when we look at our God-given role we can see that there are some GENERAL principals of how we can love people on purpose towards Jesus. And one of these principals in post-Christian Britain is TIME. Many people don't have a Christian background. Many don't know what the gospel is. Many have preconceptions about Christians being hypocrites or judgemental. And so, many people are NOT ready for you to read them John 3v16 and say "yes please, I'd like to pray the sinners prayer!"

For most people around us, having time on their journey towards faith is so crucial. And such an important way for them to spend this journey time is around you – a Christian who spends time with them, loves them, has the Holy Spirit living in you, and in the background is praying for them!

We'll consider what some of the steps you can take are in the rest of this section.

17

DON'T PREACH IT BROTHER!

Always be prepared to give an answer to everyone who asks you to give the reason for the hope that you have. But do this with gentleness and respect, so that those who speak maliciously against your good behaviour in Christ may be ashamed of their slander.

1 Peter 3v15-16

Don't preach! How's that for a surprising 2-word sentence in a book about Outreach?

I realise this chapter title is automatically going to sound controversial to some of you, so before you tear this book up and shout, "Heretic!", hear me out!

For most Christians reading this, this is probably a message you need to hear for two reasons: firstly, because you may have given up on outreach because you feel you're not able to preach, and secondly because for most people in our lives the thing that will draw them towards Jesus ISN'T us preaching to them but us intentionally loving them towards Jesus.

The reality is, most people are NOT waiting for you to share the gospel with them. We inherently know this is true, don't we? And so we can potentially fall into one of two opposite camps: either pushing on regardless like someone with a hot potato gospel, desperate to release it from our hands, or we can pull back from saying anything about our faith, perhaps with a sense of relief that the pressure is off but deep down feeling guilty about it.

These verses written by Peter, one of Jesus' closest disciples, can really help us in working out where the balance really should lie. Remember, it was Peter who knew perhaps more than anyone what it was like to blow it with Jesus, who also then experienced being forgiven and restored by Him on the beach one sunny morning over breakfast. And it was Peter who, seeing the opportunity and seizing the moment, stood up and preached on the day of Pentecost, seeing 3,000 people turn to Christ and get baptised on that incredible first day of Jesus' new church!

So, Peter's a safe pair of hands to let us know WHEN and HOW we should share our faith, and what he tells us here in 1 Peter 3v15-16 is really interesting as well as really releasing!

It feels like it starts with great pressure; this is how I've read verse 15 previously: *"Always be prepared to give an answer to everyone about the reason for the hope that you have."* These are the words my brain has taken in – and it feels like we're being told we need to share our faith non-stop, no excuses!

But the verse is actually slightly but significantly different to how I've previously read it, as it includes a few words that I hadn't taken in, which transform Peter's instructions for us…

*"Always be prepared to give an answer **to everyone who asks you** to give the reason for the hope that you have."* Those few words make all the difference, don't they! Give an answer to everyone who asks you. Not – cold call everyone. Not – go up to strangers. Not – hear someone talk about the lovely sun and respond with, "Can I tell you about God's lovely Son?"! Instead, be prepared to answer when someone asks.

You can tell Peter isn't writing these words to frontline evangelists like the apostle Paul, who was going out to city after city, preaching in town squares to anyone and everyone. Instead, Peter is writing these words as an encouragement to "normal Christians" like you and me, aware of our nervousness, aware of us feeling like we don't know enough, aware of our desire to swerve faith conversations where possible!

Be ready to share Jesus' impact on your life but wait to be asked. And when you do answer, "... *do this with gentleness and respect.*" (verse 16). Not a sales pitch, but sharing person to person, gently and in love. He's not even telling us to recite Bible verses; instead to share our experiences. This feels do-able, doesn't it? You may not be an evangelist or a preacher, but you can share what's happened to you: you can share your story!

What are they asking? Are they wanting to know about my faith? Are they asking what difference Jesus has made in my life?

No? Then don't feel like you need to preach it brother!

Yes? Then, again don't preach it! Instead, tell your story, gently and respectfully!

Don't barge in. Don't force-feed your beliefs on someone. Wait to be asked. And speak with gentleness and respect. Phew. That's a big relief!!!

Now, let's just consider what these 2 verses are NOT. They're not an excuse or a get-out-of-jail-free-card that tells us "Don't worry, if no-one ever asks, you get away with it and don't ever have to share." Jesus is our greatest treasure, isn't He? So, never ever sharing Jesus with someone could be likened to burying your treasure in the ground, which Jesus spoke strongly against in Matthew 25v14-30. We've got a life-changing message about the most wonderful

Saviour – and it's a message that people all around us NEED! And as we've seen through this book, there are lots of ways you and I can help someone begin to become receptive and interested in the message of Jesus.

But we're being reminded here to consider the feelings of the person in front of us. Honour them, respect them, act with gentleness not as a bull in a china shop!

These verses explain to me why Alpha is such an incredibly helpful place for a non-Christian to go. It's obviously a place where Jesus is spoken about every week! But the culture of Alpha is such a key part of the process for people; it's possibly the only place people may have ever been where they can hear about the Christian faith, ask questions about the Christian faith, share their doubts about the Christian faith, and even tell Christians they reject the Christian faith, in a safe environment without them feeling they're being preached at or told they are wrong. An Alpha small group is a place where gentleness and respect are high values, and listening to what the guests are feeling is more important than what the hosts may want to say. And in that context of gentleness and respect doubters, sceptics and even self-confessed atheists discover small shoots of faith begin to grow.

We'll come back to talking about Alpha in the chapter, *"Be an Alphaholic!"*

I met Nick at a toddler singing group. I really didn't want to be there! But Sarah, a mum who is part of Welcome Church who was at the group the previous week, asked me to go and take my son Ethan so I could meet Nick and his son. She'd met them the previous week. He was a stay-at-home Dad frustrated with the fact that all other stay at home parents he had met were Mums who weren't keen to hang out with a Dad and his son, which is understandable but meant the two of them never had anyone to spend time with. He felt stuck and disheartened in a new town.

It was my day off, and I reluctantly went.

It was everything I'd feared. A dusty church hall full of Mums and badly sung nursery rhymes.

Nick was actually a really good bloke, easy to get on with. We both laughed together as we endured the session and the cheap coffee! And at the end it was natural to arrange to meet up. Our boys were the same age, we lived near each other, and we could meet up next Thursday, my day off with Ethan.

Over the next few Thursdays, we hung out, we walked, we chatted, and the boys had adventures. And I intentionally didn't share my faith. Nick had mentioned that faith wasn't something he was interested in – he only went to church for weddings or funerals – so I didn't want to throw it randomly into the conversation. *"The right time will come, be patient,"* I thought.

After a few weeks, faith came up. Nick shared his scepticism and negative view of churches, I gently shared that I'm a Christian. Nick was surprised, the conversation was fine, but didn't last too long. It seemed that me being a Christian gave him a new version of what being a Christian is – I think that was a good thing!

The following month, our church had our big building launch, which you can read about in Part 4 of this book. I thought, if Nick and his family could just come, they'd love it and it would undo so many of his negative preconceptions about Christianity. My pitch was, "Come to church for our launch. I think you'll really enjoy it. And even if not, you'll get good coffee and a doughnut for brekkie when you arrive – and it's lunch back at ours afterwards!"

After umming and aahing for a few days, they agreed and came along – and LOVED IT! At lunch afterwards, they both kept saying how inspiring it was and how friendly everyone was. Nick's a musician, so he said how impressed he was with the music. And he mentioned the doughnuts a few times! *"I might just come again next week to have breakfast!"* he told me. Do you know what that was? That was someone who had a great church experience finding a low-key way of saying, *"Invite me again!"*

They came to church for most of the next 5 weeks, as well as coming to both of our midweek Toddler sessions. We'd planned our Alpha Course to begin 6 weeks after our building launch – so I invited Nick. Keeping the invite light, with the promise of more good free food and drink, he agreed to give it a go. He was starting to really connect with a church and investigate a God he didn't believe in!

Something to think about … What may have happened if I'd pushed my beliefs into the conversation too early? Would someone who had previous negative feelings or experiences about Christians respond well if I had barged in and shared my faith quickly? What does Nick's story tell us about people and faith? Perhaps people are more open than we had previously thought, if we can just look to share our lives, building authentic friendships and make an invite!

In a relationship there will come a time when your friend asks you directly about your faith, giving you permission to share, and Peter encourages us to be ready for that: *"Always be prepared to give an answer to everyone who asks you to give the reason for the hope that you have"*. And as we'll discover in the next chapter, one of the best ways to explain your faith in Jesus isn't necessarily by quoting scripture after scripture but sharing your story.

18

MEET THE FAMILY

God sets the lonely in families.

Psalm 68v6

One area of mathematics is probability, which can be simply defined as, "What are the chances of *x* happening?" For example, if I were to roll a dice, there is a 1 in 6 chance of rolling a 6.

But what are the chances of rolling six 6's in a row? Yes, you've got it – the answer is *"not much chance!"* The mathematical answer is actually 1 in 46,656 attempts. You wouldn't (or shouldn't) bet your house on it happening.

Did you know that to your friends you being a nice person may just seem like a matter of chance – in every town or street there's always one or two people who are nice, and you happen to be that one. They probably have no idea that you're nice not because you were born that way, but because God's love is in you.

The Bible reminds us of this: *"God has poured His love into our hearts by the Holy Spirit, whom He has given us."* (Romans 5v5)

So, how do you help your friends see that what they're experiencing is God's work?

One key thing is to introduce them to other Christians. As you do this, they will experience something which is statistically unusual, a bit like throwing six 6's; they will experience person after person in the same group who are *all* nice, who *all* care, who *all* love others in ways that tend to stand out from the crowd. It will cause your friend to begin to wonder, and many will begin to investigate your faith for themselves. Let me share some stories to show this.

Karen is amazing at building community on the school gate. One of the many mums she has built a friendship with is Yolanda, who wasn't a Christian, but after trying church one Sunday decided she wanted to keep coming, not because of the messages about Jesus but because of the people she met there! Karen, Yolanda and other friends were out for a meal one evening, when the subject of Christianity came up. When one of the friends asked what was so special about Welcome Church, it was Yolanda who jumped in to answer:

"The people I've met at Welcome Church care and are different to other people I've met. They are amazing people, I've always felt welcome and accepted. These people are different! I'll tell you why they're different – they actually give a ****!"

Don't be offended when I say that this may be one of the best descriptions of Jesus' church I've ever heard. In a world of 'every man for himself', Yolanda has experienced something significantly different. She'd gone from knowing Karen cared for her and made a difference in her life, to experiencing this same thing en masse; a whole church who loved and cared in ways that made a difference as she came week after week to Welcome Church.

It was probably a full 18 months later that Yolanda spoke to me in a church meeting: *"Dub, can you help? I've decided, I want to start my faith journey!"* Yolanda since signed up for our next Alpha, ready to get to know Jesus.

I knew John from the school gate. I invited him and his son Benjamin to the Welcome Church "Summer Social" – a BBQ with lots of entertainment for the kids. John describes that day as, *"the best day of mine and Benjamin's year!"* They had loads of fun, and he was amazed at how many people he met were kind, warm and friendly. John and Benjamin were the last to leave.

This inspired John to want to go to church the following day so he could meet more people, and this was the beginning of a journey of faith, leading to him doing Alpha, becoming a Christian and getting baptised. Just weeks before, he had felt so alone that he was looking up the postcode for Beachy Head, the UK's number one suicide spot. Now he was saying, *"I've not had a circle of friends before, in fact not even a short line of friends. But I've now got so many friends within Welcome Church!"* His encounter with a friendly and caring group of Christians was the catalyst to starting a journey of faith that has begun to transform his life.

Drawing people to God is not meant to be a solo experience. Jesus sent the disciples out in pairs. Life Groups and Sunday meetings are great places where Christians can grow in their faith, and not-yet-Christians can begin to connect and start a journey of faith (see Acts 2v42-47). When we help friends who are not-yet-Christians to connect to others within our church family, these new relationships can quickly lead to a new level of spiritual interest.

A COMMUNITY OF CARE

Tanya and I are part of a Life Group that we call Pudding Club. Not everyone in Pudding Club comes to the church or is a Christian. In Pudding Club there are lots of people who are going through all sorts of things, from some really big things like bereavement and serious health issues to other challenges such as job losses and family problems.

One thing that is so precious within Pudding Club is the community of support that is given. When Becca lost her job and Charlotte faced a traumatic situation in her job as a paramedic, there were loads of group WhatsApp messages offering support, encouragement and prayer. This is a typical reaction across the group to whatever is going on in someone's life.

Simon was pretty new to Pudding Club; we met him through one of the group, and we were beginning to get to know him. He was slowly showing signs of being more open to Christianity, even signing up to do Alpha. All of a sudden, as Alpha was beginning, he was rushed to hospital and needed some major operations on his foot as a result of a leg injury coupled with his diabetes. In total Simon spent four weeks in hospital having some major operations on his foot, and although people in the group didn't know Simon that well, the support he received was amazing.

Continued messages of encouragement as well as gifts from the group lifted him during the hours, days and weeks sitting in his hospital bed. Presents and cards kept him busy. As he sat in his hospital bed the night before a planned operation to remove his foot, the prayers were flowing. There were specific things prayed for to counter the issues he was facing, including prayers for blood flow to increase, for the infection to go and for God to save his foot.

"As we operate tomorrow morning, be prepared to lose your right foot," were the words of the surgeon rolling around Simon's head as he tried to get some sleep.

The next morning Simon was taken into theatre, and when he came round in recovery he was amazed and relieved to see he still had both feet! When the doctor came to see him he told him that since the previous night the blood flow had increased, the infection had gone and Simon's foot was staying where it was!

Pudding Club as well as Simon were over the moon! He was able to leave the hospital with two feet, which was pretty important for a long-distance lorry driver! But he also left hospital knowing the amazing love and support of his new Life Group 'family'.

We continued to all spend time together, do life together, and support each other in the big and the small. Simon soon signed up to do Alpha. And before long, Simon was baptised having come to faith in Jesus!

As people encounter your kindness and love in the big and the small things in their lives, they're encountering God's love through you. And it makes the world of difference.

My brother-in-law, Clint, his fiancée, Magda and their daughter came to our recent Pudding Club BBQ. It was great for Clint and Magda to get to know some of our friends from church better. Magda was heavily pregnant, so received a lot of attention! Two weeks later, Maga gave birth to their 2nd child, and Tanya was quick to message Pudding Club with the news. Helen, who leads the group with her husband Kirk, suggested a meal rota to take the burden off Clint and Magda. Within a day, 2 weeks' worth of meals were arranged, and day after day Clint would open the door to someone else from our church dropping off a lovely feast with a big smile. Clint's message to us was, *"Wow!!! I mean this is incredible and so damn lovely I could cry... We are eating like kings! I have to say it's been amazing and so helpful. What a lovely bunch of people, we are so touched!!!"*

What an extravagance for Helen to arrange this meal rota, and what an amazing act from different people – including 1 or 2 who hadn't actually met Clint & Magda! What a difference it makes for Christians to reach out and meet a need – revealing the love of God as a result!

This chapter is pretty packed with stories, isn't it? I wanted to encourage you about something which is overwhelming in its reality – when someone goes from meeting one Christian to meeting a Community of Christians, the impact really can be life-changing! We'll expand on this further in our next chapter, *Relational Momentum.*

19

RELATIONAL MOMENTUM

They broke bread in their homes and ate together with glad and sincere hearts, praising God and enjoying the favour of all the people. And the Lord added to their number daily those who were being saved.

Acts 2v46-47

Drawing people to God is not meant to be a solo experience. We see in the gospels that Jesus sent the disciples out in pairs. And as we saw in our previous chapter, introducing your not-yet-Christian friends to others from your church, so they can experience God's love and friendship through not just one person but a community of Christians, will lead many people from no interest in faith to thinking, *"I want to find out more"* about the God you follow.

John Burke, in his book Unshockable Love, refers to this process as 'Relational Momentum': gaining new Christian friends, experiencing more of God's love through His Church family and being drawn towards wanting to find out more about the God their new friends believe in. John explains that there are three elements people often need to find faith:

1. **A friendship with someone who acts like Jesus** – that's you!
2. **A relationship with other Christians whom they enjoy hanging out with and who make them feel like they belong** – your other Christian friends, perhaps your Life Group.

3. **A 'come as you are' learning environment** where they can learn, usually for 6 to 18 months, about the way of Jesus. We run Alpha followed by the Bible Course (by the Bible Society) and Prayer Course (by 24-7 Prayer). Most who do Alpha with us develop a level of spiritual interest which causes them to say yes to these next steps, and these next steps are proving really significant in people's ongoing spiritual journeys.

It's worth pointing out here that taking someone along a programme of connections is absolutely no guarantee of leading them to faith. Faith is a gift of God: it's not something we will ever be able to generate for others. At times we can help people make growing connections with our church and they reject our faith, whereas others seem to go from nowhere to faith without any of these 'Relational Momentum' steps. But we are seeing time and time again the huge difference for people in and around our communities of 'Meeting the Family' and experiencing a 'Community of Care' in helping them go from 'closed' to 'open' to hearing about Jesus. In our culture, 'Relational Momentum' so regularly makes a difference in people beginning to become receptive towards Jesus.

Burke's explanations of these elements brought real clarity to me about why some people in my life have shown a level of interest in my faith but haven't moved forward in their own journey, whereas others – including many who initially seemed a long way from faith – grew spiritually interested and over time came to follow Jesus.

One of the keys for me was understanding the importance of number two - introducing them to other Christians who they can enjoy hanging out with and who help them feel like they belong. The 'Relational Momentum' of a group of a few Christians really can make a world of difference to someone beginning to open up to things of faith.

Tanya, me, and the kids were invited to a BBQ at Matt and Bridget's house. This couple were becoming friends of ours from the school gate as their 2 girls were in our 2 oldest kids' classes. Matt and I were chatting, beer in hand, while he was cooking a BBQ. The conversation came up about my job, something that hadn't come up before then. I said, *"I'm a pastor at a church in Woking,"* to which Matt replied, *"I'm an atheist and I hate people talking about their beliefs."* Tumbleweed moment …!

In that moment I felt God say to me, *"Zip your mouth and just be friends."* Which was exactly what Matt was saying too! So I opened him another beer and mentioned how good the Braai he was cooking looked. God also whispered to me, *"And I'll save him."* Erm, are you sure God? You may have got that wrong…!

Over the next few months, we continued to hang out together as families along with Kirk, Helen and their girls. We all enjoyed each other's company. When the World Cup began in June, I invited a few dads and families from the school gate, including Matt, plus a few friends from church to three World Cup BBQ's. We drank beer, ate burgers, and cheered as England actually won some games!

Matt, Bridget and their girls then joined us at the church Summer BBQ in early July; lots of fun, very relaxed, and no preaching. Off the back of these connections with other Christians who Matt realised were normal and good to hang out with, he agreed to come to Bears Camp (a dads & kids camping weekend) with his girls, along with me and Kirk and our kids. The camp was great fun and a good opportunity for Matt to spend time with more of the dads from church.

In August we held a Pudding Club BBQ and invited Matt and Bridget. His Mum was over from South Africa, so she came too. They had a great time, and more friendships with normal Christians were beginning.

I wouldn't have been able to articulate it in this way at the time, but Matt and Bridget were benefitting from Relational Momentum; meeting and enjoying hanging out with several other Christians.

When his girls asked him to take them to church so they could go to Welcome Kids Matt eventually cracked and brought them along one Sunday in September. When I told him I was surprised to see him, he replied, *"I don't want to be here. I'd rather be anywhere else than here. But my girls have been nagging me to bring them."* My reply, *"Well, it's good to see you Matt. Let me grab you a coffee."*

After a couple months of tentatively sitting in church and hanging out with us, Matt began to connect further with Pudding Club, which consists of a mix of six 'long term' Christians and 10 new or not yet Christians. We would eat together, laugh together, and support anyone who was struggling.

Matt then decided to do Alpha at Welcome Church in February (another surprise for me!), as his caution about Christians continued to drop and his interest in Christianity started to gently grow. During an Alpha night he said, *"Everyone in this church is so nice; there must be something in it."* He was experiencing God's love through His Church, and it was making an impact. We saw earlier how Jesus told us, *"You are the light of the world."* Matt was experiencing how brightly a group of Christians shine together!

His story continued when their family came to a Bible camp with us, encouraged by a few of his new-found friends from Pudding Club who were also going to 'brave it' and come for the first time.

On the Friday morning of that camping weekend, we chatted and I encouraged him to try the 'Just Looking' seminar – for those who were still looking at and considering faith. He went and found it interesting and helpful. He attended the Saturday and Sunday sessions too, and in that final session decided he wanted to 'pray the prayer' to ask Jesus into his life. I'll let Matt tell the story from here. These are a couple of messages he shared on the Pudding Club WhatsApp group afterwards – shared with his permission:

"I asked God to come into my life during my Just Looking seminar, something I had done before. Except this time I owned it and put my hand up when asked. That was the start of the emotional overload. I stood up and left. The table host and pastor both asked if I was okay, but I could not talk, I just walked out. As I left the pastor said, "Congratulations, you are a Christian now." That really hit me hard. So I wandered back to camp not saying anything at first, trying to compose myself, scared I might start crying at some point. I can feel the welling up inside as I type this. The meeting that evening was insane, as I sang I couldn't hold back the tears. The words to the songs which I had sang before were different now, they really spoke to me. I can't type any more."

"Crazy! I was a very happy self-proclaimed atheist. I still have loads of questions but now I believe."

What followed was a mass of excited replies from the whole group, sharing our excitement at what God has done in Matt's life, to which Matt replied, *"Thanks for the kind words everyone, you have all played your part in helping me want to become a Christian."*

At our church camp, Matt's life changed in a moment. But the truth is there was a journey that led to a moment. And that journey began, how? Not by me preaching at him, that would have caused him to run a mile. Instead his journey began by being introduced to a growing number of people who were Christians that he became friends with and simply did life together with.

I later found out that lots of people in Matt's life, as he grew up, were Christians and he continually felt they were trying to force Christianity down his neck. He didn't want a Christian salesman, instead he needed genuine friends who were Christians. And as we and others 'Did Life' together, without preaching about our beliefs, little by little Matt became receptive to the message.

You can imagine our joy when Matt got baptised!

As we help people in our lives find connections with other Christians, they will be experiencing 'Relational Momentum' too, which is the doorway that God so regularly uses to instigate Spiritual Momentum. When this happens, we will begin to see God do what only God can do: touch hearts and change lives right before our eyes, which is the most precious thing on earth.

QUESTIONS:

Who are you doing life with that you can introduce to other friends from your church?

What are the natural connecting points for you to bring your not-yet-Christian and Christian friends together?

What are the things that your Life Group can do to begin to create 'Relational Momentum' with those around you?

If you're part of a Social Action ministry, what are the things you can do with those you care for to help them begin to experience 'Relational Momentum' with other people or groups within the church?

20

THE POWER OF A STORY

"Return home and tell how much God has done for you." So the man went away and told all over town how much Jesus had done for him.

Luke 8v39

Everyone loves a story. Stories cause the imagination to flow and are one of the best ways of connecting with someone else's life. Hearing someone's story helps me understand them and their life better including what their motivations are, what makes them tick, what their values are. And because it's a personal reflection, you can't argue with a story.

At Alpha, I was convinced that the favourite part of every guest's experience was me hosting and giving some of the talks. Incredibly, it wasn't! After every single Alpha Course, the most common feedback to the question, *"What did you enjoy most about Alpha?"* was the answer, *"The interviews,"* which are where we ask someone from Welcome Church about the impact Jesus has had on their life. Hearing me preach paled into insignificance compared to the inspiration guests felt as they heard someone share their story.

Lots of us find it hard to share our faith, but we can all share a story. That's the big reason our church created "Welcome Stories,"[6]

---

[6] Watch some for yourself at www.welcomestories.uk

a series of short and powerful video testimonies of God's life-changing impact on people who are part of Welcome Church. As we built up towards our building launch, we put a new Welcome Story onto our Social Media channels every fortnight. Every single one of our 14 Welcome Stories had more views and interaction online than any other post we've ever produced.

And when we played a Welcome Story each Sunday when we launched our new building, each Welcome Story stirred emotions and caused people to lean in. It wasn't just the free doughnuts that brought our friends back each week. Everyone loves a story. You can hear more about the role our Welcome Stories played in our building launch in Part 4 – "Our Story at Welcome Church".

Jesus knew that stories were important. He so regularly spoke in parables, and in the above verse his instruction wasn't to go and recite all of the verses of the Old Testament, but instead for the man to go and share his story: *"Return home and tell how much God has done for you."* Go and share your story. And the man's response was basically, *"Sure!"* He wasn't a theologian, he didn't first disappear to bible school to get a theology degree. He just went away and told people what had happened – '... *So the man went away and told all over town how much Jesus had done for him.'* (Luke 8v39).

As you connect and build life with people around you, the time will come when you'll be asked about your faith. The question is, how will you respond? To answer that, perhaps a good question to think about is, *"What are they asking for?"*

Occasionally, the answer they're looking for is chapter and verse from the Bible. But in my experience what most people most often are asking is more personal, *"Tell me of the difference faith in God has made in your life."* Or to put it more simply, *"Tell me your story!"*

So how do we do that? How can we share our story of Jesus' impact on our lives in a way that is not weird but is helpful and causes others to lean in?

Firstly, just be yourself. I've seen some people get a bit "religious" when sharing their story – sort of feeling they need to have the "right" answers or shoehorn enough bible verses into what they say. And I've seen others feeling like they need to be extra wise because they're going to be speaking about God. Some even change their voice to try to "sound" holy – whatever that sounds like!!

Just be yourself! God has made you to be you, not anyone else. And it's YOU that has this relationship that has led to the other person asking YOU to tell YOUR STORY! This is important to remember, and really liberating too. If you're someone who likes to tell jokes, be yourself as you have these conversations. Often a joke can just reinforce the fact you're "normal" as well as being someone who has faith in Jesus!

Secondly, be down to earth. Jesus who was literally from out of this world was so down to earth – He never ever spoke above someone. He used everyday language, and when describing God and faith He used analogies of everyday things that people around Him understood – sheep, farming, fishing. We're ALLOWED to be down to earth like Jesus! We're SUPPOSED to be down to earth like Jesus! If someone asked you, *"Why do you go to church every Sunday morning?"*, a true but perhaps weird-sounding answer for your friend would be *"We're the body of Christ, and it's a real priority for me to connect with other parts of the body. After all, a body needs all parts to function effectively."* Perhaps there's a more grounded and understandable answer, where we can show them we're normal, can connect with them, and can inspire them towards saying 'Yes I'll join you!'

How does this sound: *"I used to think church was stuffy and boring. But I've found being at church is such a key place for me in connecting with God. I often feel re-filled at church, ready for the week ahead."* Or, *"I love spending time with all the friends I've made at church. It's like a family, with so many people looking out for each other and caring for each other."* These types of answers may also lead to the other person's interest growing – and may lead to an opportunity to invite them – *"Why don't you come along with me this week and give it a try for yourself?"*

If you were asked why you pray, answering by sharing your confidence that God hears your prayers – and maybe to share a story of when you've seen Him come through for you will be really helpful for them to hear. It may be helpful to ground it, as well as identifying with where they may be at. For example, *"In the past I've wondered whether there's any point in praying – whether God really hears or answers my prayers. But since I've started praying more regularly, I've discovered in different instances that God does answer my prayers, and I also seem to experience a real peace when I pray."* Again, this type of conversation could easily lead to gentle follow up questions you could ask like, *"Have you ever prayed?"* and to see where that conversation goes. I think we'd so regularly be surprised and encouraged by people's responses as we ask them about their beliefs.

If I wanted to describe Alpha in a way that might help someone see why it could be good for them, I might say something like, *"I used to be confused about Jesus and his claims, but things really started to become clear when I did Alpha."* And I'd definitely mention the meals we provide in person, or how easy it is to log on to Alpha Online!

To describe my Life Group, I would focus on the fun and friendship we have, and link it to an invite: *"When I was first invited to a Life Group, I thought it would be a weird group of people sitting there in socks and sandals. But our Life Group is nothing like that! It's actually full of normal people. We have loads of fun, people support each other through all sorts of stuff – and Sarah Cake Maker always brings the best desserts you've ever eaten! Why don't you join us next week for a BBQ at ours?"*

In short, sharing your story is simple – listen, be yourself, be normal, be relevant, and where possible ask a question in response so you can get to understand more about where they're coming from. And as you do ask, remember, your role isn't to jump in here to correct wonky beliefs or tell someone they're wrong – what the other person probably most needs is encouragement. After all, they may not have been asked about what THEY believe for years (or ever!). Simply listen in order to understand, and ask questions to understand further. And you'll find you can regularly use sharing your story as an opportunity to make an invite – after all, my Life Group is fun, church is uplifting, Alpha is life-changing; what an opportunity to invite them to try it for themselves!

I'd love to just add one other dimension into this chapter – what Lois at our church calls, *"Gossiping the gospel."* This is where we don't just sit there and wait for someone to ask us to tell them our story, but instead we pro-actively drop our faith or our church into a conversation. Good news is like the fizz of champagne – it should at times just bubble over! And as we intentionally drop things into our conversations, we're giving the other person the opportunity to pick up on what we've said, or not. Sometimes people don't – they might sense you're wanting to talk about your faith and may want to avoid it. But many will respond, they will ask about whatever you've just said, giving you a green light to engage in a conversation about your faith.

You may feel that your confidence levels right now are to just wait to be asked about your story. If so, that's ok -be ready, and pray that God would open those conversations up. But as your confidence grows, you may feel ready to *"gossip the gospel"* in fun, relaxed, intriguing ways that will open up lots more conversations with lots more people.

As we close this chapter, why don't you put some time aside to write down your own answers to some of the following questions:

- *What has Jesus done in your life?*
- *What difference has knowing Jesus made to you?*
- *What prayers have you seen answers to?*
- *Why do you love going to church on a Sunday?*
- *What do you most love about your Life Group?*
- *What things did you find most helpful or inspiring about Alpha?*

As you make a note of your answers to some of these questions, and others you may think of, you're preparing yourself for those conversations where you can start to share your story in a normal, everyday way that will inspire and intrigue your friends! And as you do, don't be surprised when people pick up on what you've said, wanting to hear more – leading to all sorts of exciting conversations and lots of invites for them to come with you!

21

BE A DOOR OPENER

Better is one day in your courts than a thousand elsewhere; I would rather be a doorkeeper in the house of my God than dwell in the tents of the wicked.

Psalm 84v10

These days, when someone knocks on our front door, we open the door and stand in the doorway to greet whoever has knocked. It would be odd to open the door and hide behind it, as my children sometimes do! However, in the past, when someone knocked on the door of the Lord of the Manor, the doorkeeper would open the door like my kids. The doorkeeper had an important job – to open the door and to stand BEHIND it as he opened it, so he wasn't seen by the guest. Instead, as the guest looked into the Manor House, they would have a clear view down the hallway and would see the Lord of the Manor standing down the corridor.

Our role as Christians ultimately is to allow others to encounter Christ. Being a door opener and standing out of the way as someone sees Christ for themselves is such a helpful picture for us to have.

Psalm 84v10 helps us to see what the first and most important qualification for being a door-opener to Jesus is – and the encouraging thing is, all Christians can qualify to do it! A door-opener for Christ is someone who understands how wonderful it is to be in Jesus' presence. The Psalmist knew how precious it is to be near to God; *"Better is one day in your courts than a thousand elsewhere,"* were the words they sang in this Psalm. To love Jesus and love being with Him is the most important qualification to be a door-opener for other people to meet Him.

The other qualification flows out of this – to simply long for others to meet Jesus too! An understanding that Jesus is the only Saviour who has given Himself for the world, that He is all someone truly needs, that meeting Him is the best thing someone could ever do, all stimulate that desire in us that others would meet Him too.

I love the old-fashioned picture of us being door-openers, as it's a picture that reminds us that there's only One star of the show, One hero, One person who can transform someone's life and eternal destiny – and that's not us; it's Jesus.

We've got a God-given role to play – befriender, encourager, inviter. But our ultimate aim is for others to see Jesus for themselves, to help people come into His presence, to be transformed as they experience Him. Being a door-opener is a beautiful, God-given role where we simply help remove doors (barriers) and help people to see Jesus.

Paul & Becky had good connections to our church. Becky was a girl who grew up in the church and her husband Paul was a man who I could see God was drawing to Him. Their big issue was a deadline of needing to be out of their rented house.

What do you do in that situation? The most obvious thing seems to be to step in and help. Jesus calls us to love people in practical ways, to provide for people's physical needs as well as spiritual needs. So what could me and Tanya do? Could we give their family space in our house while they got a deposit together? Could we find some money to pay their deposit for them? Being a wannabe hero, it was my inclination to try to fix it for them. But as I sensed God's hand on their situation, I could see that my God-given role was to encourage them and pray for them but ultimately point them to Jesus and the provision He promises them.

I chatted about and prayed through Jesus' promises in Matthew 6 with them, where He told us not to worry and reminded us that God will meet all of our needs as He does for the birds of the air and the flowers of the field. I told them I believed the provision God had planned for them would be like a trophy of grace – an example they could look back at in the future and see a shining example of when God graciously provided, an example they could hold up to others too and show God's work in their lives.

Now, this was hard! It was of course very hard for them as exit day from their home approached with no sign of where they would next go. But it was hard for me as I felt I had to decide to NOT be their solution – to not be their saviour in this situation.

It just seemed clear that their journey with God THROUGH THIS would be the making of them, that it would be a foundation of the life of faith He was calling them to as a family. And it seemed vital that this challenge would point them to just one person – not Dub or another human wearing a cape, but to Jesus, God's One and only appointed hero.

My role was simply to open the door, point them towards Jesus and encourage them to believe in His provision.

The morning they were due to be out of the house, Becky called me. *"Your prayers aren't working,"* she told me, after she'd had a thoroughly demoralising conversation with the Housing Office. *"Keep praying and asking God to provide,"* I encouraged her, while helpfully telling God he needed to hurry up and solve it!

That evening, another phone call. Becky had seen a property just come up on Gumtree and had spoken to the landlord. She told her of their situation, including not having a deposit, and the landlord had replied, *"It sounds as though you need a bit of help. Come and see the house tomorrow and if you like it you can move in straight away. Oh, and no need to pay a deposit."* What a provision out of nowhere, at the eleventh hour (which seems to be God's favourite time of coming up trumps!).

They saw the house the next day and moved in immediately. Psalm 121 tells us, *"I lift up my eyes to the hills – where does my help come from? My help comes from the LORD, the Maker of heaven and earth."* (Psalm 121v1-2). If you were to ask Paul & Becky what happened, they would be able to tell you clearly, *"God provided!"* They're in no doubt as to where their help came from. What a privilege to open the door and enable Paul and Becky experience Jesus' love and provision for them. It was also a huge privilege a few weeks later as we saw Paul get baptised!

Now, this story isn't a guideline of when or how to step back from people's challenges. Regularly God's provision for people is through individual Christians or His Church, and regularly He DOES ask us to be His solution. But this story is a great reminder to us that there's only One hero, One person who we want to make front and centre, who we want to encourage people to look to above all else. And it's not me or you – it's Jesus.

So as we begin the journey of helping people come to faith, let's have this in mind. Let's be ready to be an old-fashioned door-opener, who stands out of the way so people can get to see that heaven's hero is also ready to become their hero.

22

EARN THE RIGHT TO INVITE

"Let your speech always be gracious, seasoned with salt, so that you may know how you ought to answer each person."

Colossians 4v6

So far in this book we've considered pretty thoroughly how God first wants to use you to draw people to Him, and then wants to use your other Christian friends in the process too.

The whole of the previous section ('Loving people towards Jesus') looked at how YOU may be your friends' first experience of Jesus as you do life with them; how them being around you will give them a taste of the love of God through you.

We've then considered so far in this section ('Step by Step – Loving people on purpose') how there are different steps that you can then help people make *towards Jesus*, including the 'Relational Momentum' of being introduced to other Christians so they can meet and begin to make friends with more people who are filled with the love of God.

We've ticked off 2 of the 3 parts listed in the 'Relational Momentum' chapter, which to remind you were:
1. **A friendship with someone who acts like Jesus** – that's you!
2. **A relationship with other Christians whom they enjoy hanging out with and who make them feel like they belong** – your other Christian friends, perhaps your Life Group.

Across all of this, we haven't been rushing the journey and we haven't been trying to force the Bible down their throats, but instead we've shared life with them and naturally allowed Jesus' love to shine through us. For most of us, we can feel fairly confident in both of these steps: I can be friendly and be a blessing in other people's lives, and I can introduce them to other Christians who can do the same.

While they've experienced the love of God through us and other Jesus-followers, there's still a life-changing message about Jesus that God wants them to **hear.** God's love through us may bless lives, but it's only the gospel of Jesus that transforms lives! And that's why we can never just be content with stopping at point 2; we need to help them come to Step 3:

3. **A 'come as you are' learning environment** where they can hear about Jesus, think about Jesus and over time come to faith in Jesus.

Now, I realise that while the first two steps may feel do-able, this step of making an invite may feel really daunting. I can tell that your heart is already starting to race at what may feel like a nerve-racking prospect! *"What? You want me to explain the gospel?! That's definitely beyond my pay-grade!"*

Well, I've got some really great news for you! Step 3 doesn't have to be you reciting the *'Romans Road'*[7] scriptures about sin and forgiveness through Jesus. Step 3 for most of us may well not be about **us** explaining the gospel but may instead be about us **making the right invite so others can tell them!** That's a relief, isn't it?!

---

[7] In the Bible book of Romans, Paul takes us on a journey which includes revealing our sin problem (Romans 3v23), Jesus' response (5v8 & 6v23), and the result of placing our faith in Him (10v9-10, 13)

It's worth underlining here that all our time, our love and our friendship have all earnt us something: they've earnt us **the Right to Invite**. The trust we've built over time, the fun we've had, the care we've shown, the relationship we've built, have given us this right, this opportunity, this privilege. And it really is a privilege: opening the door for others to meet Jesus is one of the greatest privileges this life affords. And as we make this invite, as we open that door, we can be confident that the God who makes all sorts of promises that He will save people, will draw many to himself through the power of His message that penetrates and wins hearts as we connect them to Him.

There are 2 key questions we can think about: *"what do I invite them to?"*, and *"how do I make a good invite?"* Let's consider the first question first – *what do I invite them to?* Well, there's no written formula here, so allow me to bring a few suggestions.

If your friend hasn't yet had connection to your church, an invite to a church social event may be a great place to start, giving them the opportunity to come and have fun with your church family in a relaxed social setting. Low-bar events like Life Group Socials, Fun Days, Fireworks Nights, Comedy Nights, Bingo Nights and Quiz Nights are all great invites to make; in fact, any event where they can enjoy chatting to Christians from your church in a relaxed social environment is ideal.

As your friend has got to know your Life Group or other friends within your church, the next step may well be an invite to come to church or to Alpha with you. At this point it's worth bearing two things in mind: your friend has become open to hearing more about your faith BUT many people have a fear of the unknown and coming to church may feel scary. The thought of crossing the threshold can feel like a big challenge, so it's really important to think through what any potential worries may be, and to alleviate them in how you make your invite – giving them the confidence to say "YES"!

You and I know that once they come, they'll feel, *"Oh, it was fine! The people were normal! The music was uplifting. The talk was interesting."* And we also know that God loves to meet people when they come into His presence. Their *"yes"* would be so exciting as the rewards for them are so high! But they won't know that until they come. And how we make our invite will make such a difference to whether they say yes or no.

So, let's consider *how we can make a good invite*. And to help with this, let's consider any fears they may have, and how we can alleviate them… Things like: *Where do I go? I don't want to turn up at a church on my own. When I arrive what happens next? Where do I park? Where do I sit? What if I can't find my friend? What if I don't enjoy it? Will my friend be offended if I decide I never want to go again?* These are genuine worries your friend may well have – all of which you can reassure them on in advance as you consider how you'll make a simple but thoughtful invite, helping to remove these barriers and go on to hear your friend say, *"Sure, I'll come!"*

"COME WITH ME!", NOT "SEE YOU THERE!"

Bearing in mind some of these potential areas of concern or uncertainty, here are a few top tips for making a good invite that makes it as easy as possible for them to say yes:

- **Be confident** … *remember, you're inviting them to something good!*
- **Be light** … *no pressure! "Come and give it a try. There is no pressure to come again if you don't enjoy it!"*

- ***Be clear*** *... what is it / when is it / when does it finish?*
- ***Be reassuring*** *... "I think you'll enjoy it, but I won't be offended if you say no, or if you come and don't enjoy it" ...*
- ***Be positive*** *... Don't say their "no" for them!*
- ***Be thoughtful*** *... "I'll pick you up" / "Let's meet out the front, we can go in together" / "come back to ours for lunch afterwards" / "We'll head to the pub to watch the game afterwards" etc.*

For someone who is in any way nervous about coming to your church, *"I'll pick you up"*, or as a minimum, *"I'll meet you out the front, we can go in together"* is so much more helpful than just sending them directions and saying, *"Here's the info, see you there"*! This may put you out – but bringing your friend to church is worth it! I remember wanting to go to church when I was 25; lots of my family were part of the church, as well as lots of family friends who I had known for years. If I had walked in, I would've known 50 or 60 people. Still, the prospect of walking in on my own was daunting – I needed someone to go in with! So when I heard my friends Ben and Tanya were going, and they said *"let's meet out the front"*, I was happy to say yes and finally cross the threshold!

Most (if not all) of your friend's initial caution will prove unfounded when they come along, so removing any areas of worry for them up front with a thoughtful and reassuring invite will help them have the confidence to say yes. A simple way to think your invite through is this: what are any potential worries or uncertainties my friend may have, and how can I help solve these by how I make my invite?

YOU COULD TRY SOMETHING LIKE THIS:

"Hey, why don't you come to church with me this Sunday? It'll be fun. I won't be offended if you don't fancy it – but I think you'll really enjoy it! All the guys we played football with will be there. We can remind Joe about the own goal he scored last week![8]

It's Sunday morning, 11 till 12.30. If we get there just before we can grab a coffee.

I'll pick you up on the way ... oh, and we'll head out to Nandos[9] *for lunch afterwards, my treat!"*

Doesn't that invite sound inviting? I don't believe there should be any other way to invite someone to something other than in an 'inviting' way – the clues in the word!

Sure, this has sometimes been done really badly. Well ... no more! We can now make good, clear, positive, helpful and inviting invitations! Our friends that we're sharing our lives with are more open to coming to church than we may think, and when we then make a clear and positive invite, we're giving them every opportunity to say yes.

I'm excited for you as you build towards your invite moments!

As you think these things through, let's look at what I think could be the BEST invite you could make – to Alpha – in our next chapter.

---

[8] Feel free to replace *"the guys you played football with last week"* with *"all of my Life Group who you met at our BBQ"* / *"the group that you met at my party"* / or wherever you've built your 'Relational Momentum'!

[9] Feel free to replace Nandos with *"to the pub to watch the game"* / *"back to mine for lunch"* / *"for a walk"* / or whatever your mutual interest with the other person is! I think you get the point!

23

BE AN ALPHAHOLIC!

So faith comes from hearing, that is, hearing the Good News about Christ.

Romans 10v17 (NLT)

I'm Dub and I'm an Alphaholic. There, I said it. Anyone who knows me will tell you this is true.

Even my 10-year-old daughter, when she asked this morning what I was writing this book about asked, *"Is it about Alpha?" "Why do you say that?"*, I asked. *"You talk about Alpha A LOT!"* was her matter-of-fact reply!

I love Alpha. I do, I just love it. I invite everyone I can onto Alpha. In this last year 14 of my friends and family have said yes to my Alpha invites.

Some people think I may need a detox. But I disagree – I want you to become an Alphaholic too. It'll do you good. More than that, it'll do the people in your life good as you make your invites and see them go on journeys of faith!

Why do I feel Alpha is such a great place to bring friends? It's because I have seen SO MANY PEOPLE come to Alpha and find themselves opening up towards Jesus as a result! I'd go as far as to say, there's NO BETTER PLACE to bring your friends, family or work colleagues who aren't yet Christians – regardless of whether they appear warm or cold to the message of Jesus.

And this is where deciding to become an Alphaholic will be such an asset to you. As we saw in the previous chapter, we're looking for a **'Come as you are learning environment'** where someone can hear about Jesus, think about Jesus and over time come to faith in Jesus. In my experience the very best invite we can therefore make is this: **Invite them to Alpha!** In our culture, Alpha really does provide a unique space. For most people, their experiences of faith conversations in the past have either been boring, irrelevant RE lessons at school, or having a discussion with a Christian that turned into a heated debate, maybe including being told they were wrong by a well-meaning but perhaps unhelpful Christian. Each of these will cause someone to feel cautious about asking or investigating in the future.

Why do people think dinner party conversations should never include religion or politics? Because so often you can be met by argumentative, rude people who are intent on shouting you down, proving you're wrong, putting their opinion in over yours.

Contrast this with Alpha, a safe space where people are ENCOURAGED to share their doubts and ask their questions about faith in a supportive environment, perhaps for the first time in their lives. No one, whatever their beliefs, will be made to look silly or told they're wrong. Everyone is listened to, encouraged and valued. This breeds confidence to discuss more and more openly as the weeks go by. The Alpha group hosts' role is NOT to convert, rather to facilitate conversations as they listen, ask questions and to seek to understand what each guest believes.

ALPHA HAS A JESUS-LIKE CULTURE – HOSTS BECOME GREAT LISTENERS

The gospels record 183 different questions Jesus was asked. Do you know how many times He answered directly? Three! And in response to these 180 unanswered questions, Jesus asked a total of 307 questions to people. Why? Was Jesus confused or unsure of what the right answers were? Was he nervous of what people would think when he revealed the truth of God to them? No! It seems that one of Jesus' priorities in these encounters was to encourage people to search deep inside themselves to work out what they truly believed.

And this is why Alpha is like Jesus – Alpha Hosts will ask questions rather than give answers, seek to help people delve deep to work out their own thoughts rather than hammer them with the right answers. Our Alpha Hosts seek to have a similar approach as Jesus by asking many more questions than they're asked. And this creates an amazing environment where people are listened to and their feelings are valued – even when the Hosts know these thoughts are very different to what the Bible says!

We've learnt over the years: let people hear the truth from the videos, listen to people's comments, ask them lots of questions to seek to really understand them and thank them for sharing during the discussion times, and watch for the Holy Spirit to be at work through the whole process. For example, a guest in my current Alpha group said on week 3 that he thought Jesus was the world's greatest illusionist. I thanked him for his comments. Yet the following week, he came back and said, *"I've thought about it – I don't actually believe that..."* – and he went on to admit he prays and thinks he may believe Jesus is who He said He was!

TWO PARTS TO AN ALPHA SESSION – HEAR THE TRUTH AND THEN DISCUSS YOUR THOUGHTS

The worry for some Christians could be that this Alpha culture of asking questions rather than giving answers could leave people with no idea about what is right, about the truth of the gospel of Jesus. The beauty of each Alpha session is the two parts of the evening: the first part is where we watch an Alpha Episode to hear what Jesus says, what the Bible says – God's truth is shared in every session. Topics like, "Who is Jesus?", "Why did Jesus die?", "Who is the Holy Spirit?", and "Why and how do I pray?" and more are covered.

The second part of the evening is where people get to share their own feelings and thoughts in light of what we've just watched. This removes every sense of the Hosts needing to persuade or argue, and instead to ask well thought out questions that cause deep thoughts and great conversations in light of the Alpha content. This creates that environment where guests know they can share whatever they think or feel, without fear of rebuke! It doesn't take long for guests to realise they CAN speak openly and honestly, in fact people are thanked for their honest scepticism!

Alpha is for EVERYONE – sceptics, atheists, nearly-Christians, lapsed-Christians. At Alpha, everyone will be listened to, everyone will be heard, and everyone will hear truths about Jesus week by week.

In this good soil of Alpha, as people begin to process and discuss their beliefs about Jesus and the Christian faith in a safe, friendly environment, the Holy Spirit ever so gently reveals the truth to people bit by bit, week by week, one person at a time. And we see all sorts of people come to faith in Jesus as a result.

I've recently been running a Bible Course group for 6 guys who have completed Alpha with us over the last 2 years, probably nearly all of which you may previously have felt would be impossible to reach with the gospel. These include a recent atheist, someone who walked away from his faith 25 years ago, a former addict, someone who rejected Christianity intellectually several years ago, a successful business owner and a millionaire. None felt like they were close to faith when they began their Alpha journey. Yet through the Alpha process of revealing Jesus alongside listening to their thoughts and beliefs, we're seeing faith grow bit by bit. And as a result some from the group will be getting wet in our baptism pool in the next few weeks!

WHAT ALPHA GUESTS ARE TELLING US

At Welcome Church, around three-quarters of those we baptise tell us that Alpha was significant in their journey to faith. We recently filmed some "Alpha Stories"[10], interviewing seven of those who did Alpha with us in the last few months to find out why they said yes to Alpha, what they were apprehensive about in advance, and how they found it when they joined us. The feedback was so fascinating and enlightening! Here are just a few of their comments:

Clint told us, *"I was worried that I'd be the one asking the tough questions or cynical questions. I was worried about being offensive, I guess. But actually, it was the opposite of what I'd expected. The hard questions were encouraged, and the conversation was good".* And he finished by telling us, *"Alpha promoted in me the start of a spiritual journey."*

---

[10] See them at www.allwelcome.uk/alpha

Anna said, *"I wasn't sure where I belonged as a single Mum and had big questions about forgiveness."* She said she got her answers to these questions on Alpha, and that *"it really helped me on my healing journey."*

Elpis wanted to reconnect with her faith and said she's since *"invited lots of people to Alpha, who have then gone on to invite their friends too! I would recommend Alpha to anyone."*

Mila said, *"I was going through personal challenges after losing different loved ones and had lots of questions about suffering. I had an emotional day at work, and my colleague invited me to come along."* Having enjoyed meeting lovely hosts who helped her feel welcome, Mila continued her Alpha journey. She explained, *"What was great about it was you could ask whatever questions you wanted, and there was no judgement."* We had the joy of baptising Mila a couple of months after she finished Alpha!

Elliott said *"No"* to his Alpha invite initially, thinking it would be awkward, before plucking up the courage to come along. He said, *"I was cynical to begin with because I didn't want to be hoodwinked into Christianity!"* After attending a couple of sessions, Elliott said, *"the discussions were the best bit. I asked quite a lot of questions and enjoyed listening to people with all sorts of different views including atheists."* After doing Alpha twice, he then thought, *"you know what, I'm going to invite my Mum along to this!"* who came to the next Alpha! Elliott got baptised nine months after first attending Alpha.

Jonathan said yes to Alpha *"because I felt like something was missing. I also quite liked the girl who asked me, so I gave it a whirl! ... Alpha brings out what you CAN do as you trust in God and His plan for you."* Jonathan is getting baptised at Welcome Church, and I married him and Jeanette (the lady that invited him to Alpha) last week!

Jean, in her late 70's, did Alpha this year. She explained, *"Life changed dramatically when my husband of 50 years died suddenly from a fatal stroke."* She realised, *"something was missing from my life, apart from John."* After saying yes to her Alpha invite, she said, *"Alpha was a real game-changer for me."* Jean's encouragement is, *"Alpha is something everybody should do. Age has got nothing to do with it, whether you're a teenager or a bit older, or an oldie like me!"* We're due to baptise Jean in a couple of weeks!

LET ME INVITE YOU TO BECOME AN ALPHAHOLIC TOO!

So many Christians seem to believe that it's the "evangelists" that are bringing people to Alpha. I've noticed that's simply not true. The main difference between a Christian that brings someone to Alpha and someone who doesn't is this – those bringing friends are doing so simply because they're the ones making the invites! They're opening up a door to a faith journey for their friend, which is an incredible thing. And so, the door is wide open for you to get involved, to be an Alpha inviter too.

If your church isn't running Alpha, what can you do? Well if you're running an alternative introduction to Christianity course, let that be your invite instead!

Are you building life with people around you and are wondering what next step invite you could make? My encouragement is to invite them to Alpha and to go with them to help them settle in. Inviting someone to Alpha is far easier than you may think, and to make an Alpha invite is to open a door for your friends to begin hearing the amazing news about Jesus. Once you've invited one or two people to Alpha, I believe it won't be long before you'll be as excited as me at the impact Alpha is making, and you'll be saying with me, *"I'm an Alphaholic too!"*

24

THE HARVEST IS PLENTIFUL

Then Jesus said to His disciples, "The harvest is plentiful but the workers are few. Ask the Lord of the harvest, therefore, to send workers into His harvest field."

Matthew 9v37-38

Both Tanya's mum and my dad are incredible gardeners. Between them they grow a huge variety of fruit and vegetables. They prepare the soil and plant seeds in the winter. They tend to their plants and crops in the spring and summer, continuing to prune and water. And then the harvest comes. You feel like you're surrounded by a bounty of the freshest, tastiest fruit and veg you can imagine! When it comes to the time to pick, my children love it! The only issue is, around 50% of what my kids pick doesn't make it into their baskets, and by the time they've finished Ethan in particular seems to be covered head to toe in seeds and fruit juices. Mysterious.

I was saying to my dad that it seems a shame that everything turns ripe at the same time. You can't eat the fruit early, and it's not a good idea to leave fruit on the vine for weeks after it's become ripe. When the time is right, you need to pick it all and tuck in!

But still, those few weeks of feasting bring us great pleasure. Harvest time is where we know that all the investing in planting, weeding, and watering were worth the wait.

It's the same with Jesus' words about His harvest, but infinitely more so because the harvest He's talking about is a harvest of lives that He is going to transform as He brings people into His family.

I wonder how Jesus' disciples felt as he spoke the words listed at the top of this chapter. They'd heard His teaching – the greatest words ever spoken. He'd taught them that God's love for the world was so great that God had sent Him into the world to save people. His incredible power had been demonstrated through amazing signs and miracles. Matthew records in Chapter 9 verse 35, *"Jesus went through all the towns and villages, preaching the good news of the kingdom and healing every disease and sickness."* The disciples, and everyone else who encountered Him, had never witnessed anything like it.

And they'd personally experienced Jesus' incredible love for people, which was the foundation for everything He did. In verse 36, Matthew notes this; *"When He saw the crowds, He had compassion on them, because they were harassed and helpless, like sheep without a shepherd."* Jesus didn't need to TELL His disciples how He felt about the people He was encountering because His feelings of love and compassion spoke a thousand words. There's nothing on earth like seeing Jesus reach out and transform people's lives, and the disciples got to witness it first-hand.

Jesus then speaks the words written at the top of this chapter: *"The harvest is plentiful, but the workers are few."* My guess is they had no idea whatsoever of the world transformation that Jesus was going to bring about out of this promise of a plentiful harvest. Perhaps the disciples were thinking, *"Maybe Jesus is going to save another few people, maybe many people, maybe even a few thousand!"* But as we look across the world today research estimates that over 2,300,000,000 people (yes, over 2.3 *billion!*) say they have been impacted by Jesus' power and love and have become His followers.

He spoke this truth, *"The harvest is plentiful,"* over Jerusalem and the villages and towns around it. He speaks this truth over Woking and the surrounding area, and He speaks this truth over the people He's placed around your life too.

As Christians, we believe that this man Jesus, who walked the earth two thousand years ago, was brutally killed on a Roman cross yet overcame death because God the Father raised Him to life again. We believe that He saves and forgives people today, and we believe that He continues to personally impact our own lives. These are all incredible claims that we have come to place our faith in. In light of us believing these astounding truths, why is it that when we hear Jesus say, *"The harvest is plentiful,"* our reaction can often be unbelief, apathy or indifference? We respond, *"I'm too busy" "I'm just not that bothered" "Nah, not around here Jesus. It's tough around here; no one is interested."*

Let's just pause for a moment and think about this. The God of Heaven came to earth. He spent time with twelve followers, and the numbers grew a little. He then claimed that *"the harvest is plentiful."* He also said to His followers, *"You will do greater things than me."* After He rose from the dead, He gave His Holy Spirit to empower every one of His followers with the same power and authority He had. And since then, the numbers of Christians has spiralled to a simply mind-boggling level. Research estimates that around 174,000 people become Christians every day? That's 63 million people this year! That would be more than 1 billion people in the next 16 years! Some of these He's placed around you.

If you've ever wondered why Jesus hasn't wrapped this world up yet and taken all of His followers to be with Him, this is the reason: He continues to be on the greatest mission on earth to seek and save millions upon millions of people. Jesus is fulfilling His promise that the harvest is plentiful because He is the King of Heaven who loves people and is passionate about bringing them into His family!

So, when Jesus says, *"the harvest is plentiful,"* He's speaking to you and me, right here, right now, where we live. He then goes on to say, *"but the workers are few. Ask the Lord of the harvest, therefore, to send workers out into His harvest field."*

It's not a surprise to Jesus that 90% of Southern Baptists say they're never going to share their faith with anyone else ever. And it's not a surprise to Him that most Christians in our churches have written themselves out of His primary mission on earth too. But I believe it's something of great sadness to Him, which is what stirred Him to encourage us to see the harvest, to see the tiny number of workers in His harvest, and then to ask us to pray to Him to send people into His harvest field.

So why don't we do that now?

Lord Jesus, thank you that you have created a huge harvest, and are continuing to reap your harvest in huge numbers every single day. Thank you that this is because of the great love and compassion you have for people all around us. Please send many more workers into your harvest field where I live. Amen

That's a great prayer to pray to Him. It shows our heart's desire for our friends and loved ones to encounter Jesus. And as we do so and sit quietly in His presence, perhaps we can hear His response ...

"I'd love to. Can I send you?"

As we consider our response to His call on us, let's look at His promises to us of what we can expect the fruit to be if we step into His harvest field. That's what the next chapter is about.

25

YOU'RE FRUITY!

'I am the vine; you are the branches. If you remain in me and I in you, you will bear much fruit; apart from me you can do nothing … this is to my Father's glory, that you bear much fruit, showing yourselves to be my disciples … My command is this: love each other as I have loved you. Greater love has no one than this: to lay down one's life for one's friends. You are my friends if you do what I command. I no longer call you servants, because a servant does not know his master's business. Instead, I have called you friends, for everything that I learned from my Father I have made known to you. You did not choose me, but I chose you and appointed you so that you might go and bear fruit – fruit that will last – and so that whatever you ask in my name the Father will give you. This is my command: love each other.

John 15v5, 8 & 12-17

I believe this can be a really defining moment for you and me right here.

We've looked at Jesus' call on us to fulfil the Great Commandment to love. We've seen through lots of stories how leading with love is often the catalyst to God stirring up a spiritual interest and openness in people. We've just looked at Jesus' promise that the harvest is plentiful. And we've considered His heart as He says to us, *"I want to send you."*

But what can we expect if we respond? After all, what effect can we possibly have? No one's going to listen to us! I couldn't save a penalty, let alone a human soul. I can't even save myself.

And that's where Jesus wants to speak to us from the above verses. He says in summary, *"If you're connected to me and love others in sacrificial ways, you will produce the fruit of lives transformed by me that will last into eternity!"*

Isn't that just the most incredible promise? And the key thing for us to notice is this: the work of life transformation will be done **BY JESUS THROUGH US** because we are connected to Him! This commissions every single one of us to see ourselves as workers in Jesus' harvest field. He has a role for each of us to play in seeing people come to know Him. He will work through each one of us if we let Him.

I can love others in sacrificial ways because Jesus' sacrificial love has been poured into my heart. And as I do, the Lord of the harvest will draw people to Him, producing MUCH FRUIT. The upshot is this **– JESUS HAS DESIGNED YOU TO BE FRUITY!**

I love it when my dad or Tanya's mum delivers us a big bright bowl of freshly picked fruit and veg. Let's picture the time when you will come face to face with Jesus. Isn't it an amazing thought to be able to bring Him a great gift – fruit of us playing our part in seeing lives transformed in His harvest field! He calls you into His harvest field and promises you will reap lots of fruit as you go.

In Daniel 12v3, God paints a beautiful picture of the eternal rewards He has for all of us who lead others to faith in Jesus: *"Those who lead many to righteousness will shine like the stars for ever and ever."* Isn't that beautiful? Isn't that a picture to savour? And doesn't that reveal the level of importance God is placing on us leading people to Him?

THE FRUIT IS WORTH THE FRUSTRATION!

It's important to face this reality – this whole-life calling of loving people towards Jesus won't always go smoothly, and won't always result in every person coming to faith in Christ. I could give you a long list of frustrations, sadness and disappointments – of some just rejecting Jesus from the outset and of others appearing to come to faith only to disappear out of the back door before you know it. If you make the decision to live your life loving people towards Jesus, you'll have lots of disappointments along the way.

BUT …! The joy of seeing ONE PERSON coming to faith in Christ is so amazing, so wonderful, such a privilege that every turned down invite, every single frustration, will be worth it. I can tell you hands down that the fruit is worth the frustration!

I met Sarah and her husband Harry four years ago. Cancer had returned to Harry for the third time, and this time the doctors said it was terminal. As Dean and I went to visit them at their home we encountered an extremely sick man. Through a conversation about peace with God both now in this life and on into eternity, Harry said that he wanted to know this peace. We explained that it was Jesus who offers this peace, and Harry decided to pray to ask Jesus to come into his life. As I finished praying this prayer with Harry, energy seemed to flood into his body as he said Amen with great conviction. In an incredible moment at the end of his life, Harry prayed a prayer to Jesus, who received Him with great joy!

The following day, Harry was taken into a hospice, and he died a week later. He met his Maker who had become his Heavenly Father just a few days earlier.

We kept in touch with Sarah, looking to continue to support her. She decided a month later to sign up for Alpha. Beyond that, she and others from our Alpha table still had questions, and we began "Alpha Pudding Club," where we'd meet each week at our house, continuing to build friendships and help them on their journeys of faith.

As she began to come to church with us on a Sunday, tears would pour down her face during the worship as God gently and tenderly met with her deep down and began a process of revealing His love and healing in her. I remember the joy I experienced as Sarah told me she had become a Christian!

This is just one story of Jesus working in people's lives. There are many more I could share, because Jesus is continuing to fulfil His promise that His followers will produce much fruit.

Let me warmly encourage you to remain close to Jesus and to reach out in love to the people He's placed around you, being confident that He is at work through you and that you will produce much fruit.

BE THE REVIVAL!

As I read about revivals in days gone by, my mind is blown by what God did in transforming individuals and nations. It's hard to know what revival would look like in my town or yours, isn't it? But what a mouth-watering prospect it is to dream about seeing revival, where the presence of God is so powerful that tens of thousands of people across our towns, and millions across the UK are drawn to Jesus in a moment.

If we desire our nation to be transformed by the power and grace of God, surely that then filters down to our desire to see people right around us transformed. And if that's our heart, I think it can only lead us to one thing – action!

After all, what is one person coming to faith? It's revival in someone's life, which can lead to revival in a family or friendship group.

Jesus spoke to Paul in a vision when he was in Corinth: *"... I have many people in this city."* (Acts 18v10). It was a promise of a move of God – saying that there were many people Jesus was going to reach and save in Corinth. A revival in the city was promised to Paul!

So, how did Paul receive these words? He didn't sit there and wait, praying for a move of God. He set to action! Check out the next verse:

"So Paul stayed in Corinth for a year and a half, teaching them the word of God." (Acts 18v11)

You see, waiting for revival isn't a bed for our laziness – I'm just going to sit, pray and dream about a move of God. No! It underlines the need for us to get out there and **see revival one person at a time!**

What a great example of someone desiring to see revival! Paul **BECAME A MOVE OF GOD** by stepping out and sharing Jesus left, right and centre!

So as you and I consider Jesus' promise of building His Church, of desiring that people all around us would be saved, and promising that you and I will be fruitful as we step out of our bubbles into other people's lives, we too can **SEE A MOVE OF GOD:** we too can **BE A MOVE OF GOD!** What an exciting prospect, what an incredible promise, and what a huge motivation to get out there and love others all around us, left, right and centre, towards Jesus!

26

LOVING PEOPLE TOWARDS JESUS AT WELCOME CHURCH

"No longer do I call you servants, for the servant does not know what his master is doing; but I have called you friends, for all that I have heard from my Father I have made known to you."

John 15v15

I wrote the first edition of this book in September 2019. At the time, at Welcome Church we would see around 550 people attend church with us each Sunday across our two meetings, including children.

In the preceding two years, as an eldership team we'd spent lots of time discussing and preaching about the culture of the church, underlining an emphasis on being a church **more like Jesus**. This sounds so obvious when you read it, but we saw how easy it is for Christians to behave as if we're "holier than thou" rather than full of grace to people around us. We'd been really shaped by John Burke's two books, "No Perfect People Allowed" (Published by Zondervan) and "Unshockable Love" (Baker Books), which both highlight the huge differences between Jesus and the Pharisees as revealed in the gospels. Jesus was described by the Pharisees as *"a friend of tax collectors and sinners"* (Matthew 11v19). We reflected a lot on how churches can subtly end up more like self-righteous Pharisees rather than compassionate like Jesus, and we emphasised Jesus' call to be kind-hearted and gracious to everyone we meet.

We also worked a lot on how we can create a culture where new people that came to church felt welcomed and included rather than outsiders turning up at a members-only club. The phrase **"BELONG, BELIEVE, BECOME"** became our slogan as well as the title of one of our significant preaching series: people can come to our church and know they **BELONG** whether or not they **BELIEVE** in Jesus, and we wouldn't be expecting them to **BECOME** the person God had intended until they had come to **BELIEVE** in Jesus – after all, it's only Jesus that transforms a life from the inside out. All of this groundwork of creating a culture of BELONGING in our church was really key in giving everyone confidence that their guests would enjoy themselves and be keen to return, which in turn gave confidence for people to step out and make invites.

We were in the middle of a building project of a new, 650-seat auditorium, as well as re-shaping our current building. We wanted to create a church building that could be a hub for Woking and over time we wanted to see thousands of people come through our doors.

The launch date for the building was set – January 2020, and people across the church were really excited at the prospect of this beautiful new facility.

There were some nagging questions that were hanging over me; How can we help the church to see that this new building was as much for those NOT YET CONNECTED to our church as it was for us as a church community? How could we use this building launch as a springboard to see hundreds more people come along? How can we make the most of this God-given moment?

The culture of our church was growing more and more inviting – people who came as guests felt welcomed and lots were keen to return. But there weren't many of us making invites for people to come. There were the usual keenies that would invite friends; it was probably 10% of the church making 90% of the invites.

We needed to bring vision for this God-given opportunity, to show the possibilities of what MIGHT happen if we all got ready to make our invites. And we needed a strategy – how could we help our church make step-by-step invites as a build-up to the big Sunday launch?

WRITE A PLAN AND WRITE A BOOK!

In what felt like a heavenly download, God gave me a strategy for our church for the next few months, a vision for how we could empower people across the church into this all-play task of loving people towards Jesus, with the aim of seeing hundreds more people attend our Launch Sunday and hopefully begin a journey towards Jesus.

As this vision came together, Steve Petch our Lead Pastor encouraged me to write a book to bring this vision of loving people towards Jesus to life. I'd never considered being an author in my life, so that conversation was a bit of a surprise! But I could see how God had put something in me that I really believed would speak to our church and impact those around us as a result. So, in a crazy-busy week and a half in September 2019, version 1 of this book was written!

We gave a copy of the book to EVERYONE who was part of Welcome Church, and each Sunday would share excerpts and encouragements to read it and begin to live it. And alongside that, the journey to Launch Sunday was set out, cheesily but memorably called the **Hop, Skip & Jump!** The plan was this – as Christians "did life" with those all around us, we would have some easy invite events that the church would put on that we could all bring our friends to. One event followed another and was then followed by the bigger invite – to Launch Sunday. We underlined what you might consider as quite unusual in the Hop and Skip phases – DON'T INVITE THEM TO CHURCH! Allowing people to go on a journey towards their first Sunday was really important, and giving the right amount of time for this for each individual was key.

The **"Hop"** was a free Funday in late September. The vision was to see 500 friends come and have fun with all sorts of games, entertainment, live music, a big free BBQ and Ice Creams to follow. Sure enough, just over 500 guests were brought by people across our church. Everyone was given a lanyard on arrival – details of the schedule of the afternoon was on one side, and a sign-up form on the back to receive free tickets to our Fireworks Night in November was on the back. The atmosphere was good, people were served at all of the stalls with kindness and a smile; what a great afternoon! And out of the 500 guests, 460 signed up for free Fireworks Night tickets – all of a sudden, a one-off Funday was leading to a follow-up connection at our Fireworks Night – 2 church connection points in six weeks.

And so we headed towards the **"Skip"**. Our Fireworks Night was going to be good! Lots of money was invested in the fireworks display, and everyone would receive a free hot dog or burger and a drink on arrival. Alongside the 460 already signed up, we promoted it elsewhere, put a nominal fee on entrance, and saw a total of around 1,700 guests come in total! That included 18 families from my son's class in the crowd! I was on the gate as people left, and the feedback was overwhelming at how good the evening was, how well people felt looked after. The church was shining bright (remember Matthew 5v14-16?), and people were noticing!

PREPARING TO LAUNCH

We were now getting ready for the **"Jump"** as we headed to Launch Sunday. We were seeing people across the church really seeing the vision in their own lives – *"I've got people in my life who have attended these events – are really warm towards our church – and I'm going to find the courage to make that invite to our Launch!"*

As we prepared for Launch, we put a big challenge in front of all of our teams: How can everyone who attends have **A SUNDAY TO REMEMBER**? How can your team or ministry help someone walk away thinking, "Wow!!"? Part of our vision was hospitality – we wanted to go from tea & coffee served after our meetings to coffee, pastries and fruit both on arrival and afterwards. It required an investment, but the opportunity to bless people extravagantly was worth it.

We wanted to think everything through, from people's first contact as they parked their car to their experience as they arrived at the door, to the reception they received as they dropped their children to Welcome Kids, to the delights our Brew Crew had put together, as well as which songs our Worship Team would play, and the content of every aspect of the service.

We played Mike's Welcome Story – a powerful, emotional story of attempted suicide, deep depression, and of his life and family being completely transformed when he came to our Fun Day, followed by coming to Alpha and over time coming to faith in Jesus.

The group of friends Tanya and I brought included lots of "non-church" people, who were cautious at first. But the offer of brekkie on arrival and then lunch at ours afterwards was enough for lots of them to say, *"Go on then, I'll come just this once."* We brought 40 friends to church that day including kids – all of which squeezed into our house afterwards for lunch!

Lots of the comments back at ours were something special. *"We can't stop talking about it!"*, *"The music was so uplifting." "The coffee and pastries were so good! I'm coming again next week just to get my breakfast!"* And several did, coming most weeks until lockdown closed the building.

That Launch Sunday, our attendance went from 550 people previously to 1,250 that day. 700 extra people visited our church for our launch. Some were local dignitaries and others were previous church members who returned for the day. But around 500 of them were guests invited by people within the church!

As we sat and reviewed our Launch Sunday the following day in the office, we were all tired but exhilarated! God had revealed how we could all play our part in loving people towards Jesus and had given us some clear and easy steppingstone invites. And our vision of 1,000 people at Launch Sunday had been well and truly smashed!

We knew in advance that seeing lots of people come to the Launch would be fantastic. But helping them return was crucial – we wanted it to be the beginning of a spiritual journey for many, not just a one-off visit. So, everyone who came to the Launch and gave us their details received a Pret coffee voucher in the post that week alongside a simple note thanking them for attending and encouraging them to come again next week. These people were precious guests in our new home, and we wanted them to know it.

Launch Sunday was also Week 1 of a 6-week 'Welcome Stories' series, where we would show a Welcome Story every week alongside revealing Jesus' heart for people from the gospels. We felt that the power of our Welcome Stories would be a great draw for people to return.

The question that hung there all week was, "How many will return next week?" Will we go back to 550 people? Will **some** of them return? The following Sunday we were so excited to see 800 people come to church, and over the following 10 weeks our average attendance was 750 people. Our Launch had led to **200 MORE PEOPLE** joining us every Sunday!

We'd planned week 4 after Launch to be a Baptism Service. We baptised 15 people, all of whom shared their story on a pre-recorded video. We heard from Steve Petch as he explained how the baptism pool represented a grave (dying to our old life), a bath (being washed of our sins) and a cradle (being raised to a new life), and saw each one go into the baptism pool, and come back out with beaming smiles, many punching the air in delight! There was so much emotion in the room, including across our new attendees, as we watched 15 people sharing how Jesus has transformed their lives.

We learnt lots across our **Hop, Skip & Jump**. We learnt that having a step-by-step journey plan towards a Sunday is really important. We learnt that lots more people are open to connecting with church through us than we had believed. As many of us stepped out to make our invites, we learnt that God's heart for people and desire for them to encounter Him is extravagant and breathtaking. And we experienced the great joy of partnering with God in loving people towards Jesus!

God has an adventure for ALL OF US in seeing people come to faith in Jesus. He wants to break down the high bar of 'evangelism', and replace it with the hugely encouraging message of 'loving people towards Jesus'. This is something we are all called to **individually,** as we reach out to people all around us. And this is something we've been called to **together**, as whole churches, as we look to build 'Relational Momentum' by connecting people to God's family, His Church, and to then make the invite to Sunday mornings and through courses like Alpha, helping people step by step begin their spiritual journeys.

I hope the story of the Welcome Church **Hop, Skip & Jump** has opened your eyes to what God wants to do through **YOUR CHURCH** as you create plans and all reach out together!

27

HERE AM I. SEND ME!

Then I heard the voice of the Lord saying, 'Whom shall I send? And who will go for us?'
And I said, 'Here am I. Send me!'

Isaiah 6v8

I remember as a child visiting my Grandpa. I've got lots of great memories, but I always looked forward to one thing in particular. He would have a job that needed doing: a trip to the shops to collect his morning paper. And my brother who is eight years older than me was always the one allowed to go. A child being entrusted with this exciting adventure was a bit exciting. The extra money he was given to buy some sweets was another level!

When my Grandpa thought I was old enough, he gave me the option of going with my big bro. My response was immediate, with a big smile and without hesitation: *"Yes! I'll go!"* And off we went, straight to the shops to buy the newspaper. And a big bag of sweets.

We've now come to the final chapter and the moment to make a decision in response to Jesus' call.

In chapter 24 we looked at Jesus' statement that, *"The harvest is plentiful but the workers are few. Ask the Lord of the harvest, therefore, to send workers out into His harvest field."* (Matthew 9v37-38).

Although to reap a great harvest of lives is the Great Commission that He gave to His church, Jesus knew that lots of Christians would be reluctant to step out into this harvest field. But because of His great love for people, He encouraged us all to ask Him, the Lord of the harvest, to send out workers for Him.

We've looked at how, when we ask Him, *"Please Lord, send someone into your harvest field, to the people you've placed in my life,"* we can sense His response, *"I'd love to. Can I send you?"*

It reminds me of Isaiah's encounter with God, recorded in Isaiah chapter 6.

Isaiah has just been in God's incredible presence and experienced His forgiveness, just like you and I have done through Jesus. God has a crucial mission and is looking to send someone, just like Jesus wants to send people into His harvest field. And what is Isaiah's response? It's positive and immediate, just like a kid being given money to go and spend at the newsagent. Here's the conversation, recorded in Isaiah 6v8:

"Whom shall I send? And who will go for us?"

"Here am I. Send me!"

That's the response that Jesus is asking us to make. He's placed precious people in and around your life and mine. He promises to provide us with all we need to reach out and love them towards Him. Unlike God's call on Isaiah, God's call on us seems less on preaching judgement, and more on loving one person after another towards Him. I find that a great relief; it's something that every one of us can feel, *"I can do that!"* And Jesus promises that we will be incredibly fruitful as we go – we can ALL see people come to Jesus through us!

Ephesians 2v10 reminds us that, *"we are God's handiwork, created in Christ Jesus to do good works, which God prepared in advance for us to do."* It's been so wisely said that God has been **PREPARING US** for the works He's **ALREADY PREPARED FOR US.** Perhaps the 27 chapters of this book are part of God's preparation for you, building your faith and passion in God's desire to transform lives all around you, **THROUGH YOU.**

And so, as we draw this book to a close, Jesus wants to ask that same question that was asked of Isaiah to you and me:

"Whom shall I send? And who will go for us?"

That's the question, it's simple and significant. And maybe it's time for us to answer him. Have you committed to your answer? I've committed to mine.

"Here am I. Send me!"

QUESTIONS

As you read Chapter 16 – "Loving People on Purpose", how did you feel about the strategic nature of God? What did that show you about God's desire to draw people to Him?

How do you feel now about Jesus' claim that "the harvest is plentiful" around you? How has this book encouraged you about the plans Jesus has to transform lives around you?

Why don't you spend some time now chatting with God, telling Him how you're feeling about loving people towards Jesus, asking Him to fill you with faith, and asking Him to make you fruitful as you go. And end your prayer telling Him, *"Here am I. Send me!"*

EPILOGUE

I love listening to apologetics – where well-read theologians discuss and prove topics like the authenticity of Christianity, the credibility of the Bible, and the historicity of Jesus' life, death, and resurrection. As I listen to these people, I find it encourages me and builds me up in my faith. There are some great resources looking at some answers to the common questions and doubts people may have about Christianity.

You may have noticed that this book isn't in any way a book on apologetics, a big "how to" on answering the big questions people may have about faith. We could have spent time rehearsing some answers to the common questions people have about Christianity, so we could be poised and ready to "prove" Jesus to a sceptic when they chuck their doubts at us. That would be a great book to write – but it isn't this book.

We have talked mainly about 'doing life' with the precious people God has placed around us, and through our relationships helping them to become open step by step to hearing the message of Jesus. We've looked at how God wants to use our lives to have great impact on people all around us, and how He wants us to love people on purpose, step by step towards Jesus.

This book is really born out of two things:

Firstly, it's born out of what God has been challenging me personally, time and again, to think about. I've been deeply impacted by Bible verses like, *"The harvest is plentiful,"* and *"You are the light of the world,"* and *"Let your light shine before men that they may see your good deeds and glorify your Father in heaven."* God has been showing me how relevant these words are to **MY LIFE**, today, 2,000 years after Jesus spoke them. I've also been massively inspired by the growing reality that Jesus is going to shine His light through me.

Secondly, it's born out of what I am regularly beginning to see taking place among people who have become open to Jesus all around me. I'm hearing story after story with a common thread: so many people are beginning journeys of faith primarily because of the impact of Christians in their life who cared for them in ways that made a difference. God in His kindness has given us a method that we ALL can get involved in. No longer do we need to feel second-rate or a failure for not being an 'evangelist'. No longer do we need to feel like we need to 'qualify' to get involved in helping people come to faith. I'm wowed by God's kindness that He's given us a method in 21st Century, post-Christian Britain, that ALL CHRISTIANS – yes, including you and me – can play our part in, of loving people towards Jesus.

I'm not hearing stories of Christians debating with their atheist friends long into the night, leading to the atheist saying, *"Ok. Your arguments have convinced me. I'm ready to become a Christian."* I'm not hearing stories of people coming to faith because someone preached at them in the town centre or knocked on their door with a fake questionnaire. Perhaps people came to faith by one of these routes in the past – maybe you did, and if so that's wonderful. But it seems to me that Jesus' primary way of drawing people to Him right now in the UK is through His love shining through His followers and them making a difference in someone's life.

Of course, once God is drawing someone to Himself, we do need to gently and lovingly tell them about who Jesus is and what He has done for us. Concepts like sin, repentance, faith, forgiveness, baptism, resurrection, eternal life, and peace with God are cornerstones of our faith, and people will only know about these things if we tell them. And that's where Alpha, follow up courses like the Bible Course & Prayer Course, as well as church on Sunday mornings, play such a crucial role. But I am convinced that blunt confrontation is rarely the best starting point for people who feel far from God.

I am hearing story after story of people experiencing great friendships with Christians, enjoying introductions to other Christians and, over time, accepting invitations to church or to Alpha. 'Relational Momentum' is a method God is regularly using to draw people all around us to Him. And lots of these stories culminate with them coming to a decision to put their faith in Jesus, with a whole new life and eternity ahead of them.

Jesus, the Lord of the harvest, is asking us to love people towards Him. I hope the chapters and stories within this book inspire you to get on board with what God is wanting to do through you.

I'm incredibly excited about the adventure Jesus has for us all individually and through our churches as we respond to his call. Perhaps there are future chapters to be written of the lives Jesus is going to transform through you!